The Christian Challenge Series
Edited by ASHLEY SAMPSON

*

THE CHRISTIAN HOPE OF IMMORTALITY

THE CHRISTIAN HOPE OF IMMORTALITY

By

A. E. TAYLOR

M.A., D.Litt., LL.D

LATE PROFESSOR OF MORAL PHILOSOPHY IN THE
UNIVERSITY OF EDINBURGH

NEW YORK

THE MACMILLAN COMPANY

1947

First Printing

I

THE title we have given to these pages is meant to be an exact indication of the subject with which they are concerned; they are to deal throughout with the hope of "immortality", not with the much wider subject of the "prospect of survival after death". The distinction is all-important, because while, as we shall try to show, the hope of eternal life is the very mainspring of high religion and noble moral living, the mere persuasion of survival, however confidently entertained, has of itself no moral or religious value whatever. It is the *quality* of the life for which a man believes himself to be made that makes all the difference; there is nothing inspiring in the mere thought that one is destined to go on living, in the bare sense of being alive, for an indefinitely long time. That belief and the practices to which it gives rise we may be content to leave to the study of the anthropologists, except for a few general remarks which shall be condensed into a single paragraph or two.

In view of the familiar experience of human mortality it is at least a thought-provoking fact that the conviction that, despite all appearances to the contrary, the dead have not wholly ceased to be, but still are something and someone, should be so widespread among mankind that we may fairly call it *universal*, and again *primitive*, in the sense that it is presupposed by the funerary customs of the earliest and rudest human beings of whose habits of life we have any adequate knowledge; how it came into existence we do not know, and can merely guess; all we know is that we find it there. But it is to be observed that there is little or nothing we can recognize as ethical or religious about the earliest forms of this belief. A man's life in the hereafter is not supposed to be in any way dependent on the moral quality of the life he leads " in the body ". The dead are thought of as merely continuing to exist in the unseen world in the same sort of company in which they existed when they were among us, with, of course, the difference that the gross palpable body of flesh has been replaced by a " shade " or a " wraith ". The hunter continues to hunt, though his game is, like himself, a " shade "; the man who needed food and clothes has still the corresponding needs, though they can be satisfied by placing clothes and food on his grave, or, where cremation is the custom, by burning them there. The deceased chieftain must be attended by his retinue of wives and servants, but they have first to be killed and so sent with him to the unseen world, or their place be supplied by dummies which, like himself, are " the same thing and yet not quite the same thing ".

We are most familiar with this non-ethical and " secular " conception of the other world from its reflection in great literature belonging to an age when the original belief is already beginning to fade. The Greek " ghost " had clearly once been a cherished or a dreaded reality, as we see from the Athenian practice of annually entertaining the family dead at a solemn festival and then banishing them from the household for the coming year. But Homer's ghosts are already far on the way to being nothing at all; they can do little more than appear from time to time to the still living in their dreams. They may, indeed, be seen by a living man in the waking state if he journeys, like Odysseus, to their strange and distant land and performs the due rites of

evocation. But until they have been momentarily revivi-
fied by the taste of sacrificial blood they cannot so much
as speak and are apparently not even conscious. Their
life, if you can call it so, is a dreary and joyless automatic
repetition of their occupations on earth; above all, there
is no question of any moral retribution in the land of the
dead for deeds done in the life of the flesh. One who
has been a king or judge on earth, like Minos of Crete,
still "judges" among the shades, but it is only, like the
dead hunter's pursuit of phantom game, a dream-like
following of his old trade with no more moral significance than a sleeping hound's dream of the chase.

Much the same picture of the state of the dead is
found in all but a few of the very latest passages of the
Old Testament scriptures, as we can see from the book
of Job, or the "taunting song" on the death of the king
of Babylon which has found its way into the book of
Isaiah, as well as from many briefer utterances in the
Psalms. Those who have "gone down to the pit" are
not nothing, but their existence is as empty as it can be
consistently with being anything at all. In particular, "in
the pit" there are no rewards or punishments; moral
distinctions belong to this present life under the sun, and
end with it. The helpless state of the dead king of
Babylon is no punishment for, and no consequence of,
his old arrogance; it is the common lot of mortality, and
is shared by all the other deceased monarchs; so far as the
poet thinks of him as punished in any way, it is only by
being deprived of a magnificent royal burial; for the rest,
good and bad alike, once dead "lie in the hell like sheep".
What is more striking still, the jurisdiction of the God of
Israel ends at the grave, and the Old Testament writers,
unlike the Greeks, know nothing of any other "god
of the underworld". Yahweh is, in the most literal

sense of the word, a " god not of the dead but of the
living "; the living praise him, but there is no worship
or religion among the dead. For the Israelite, until long
after the return from the Captivity, as for the ordinary
Greek, all the real interests of man, including even the
interest of worshipping Yahweh and keeping his laws,
belong to this side of the " great divide "; what lies on
the other side is an existence so dreary and meaningless
that a man does best to keep it at arm's length so long
as he may, and to avert his thoughts from it.

In the great tradition of Christianity, as we all know,
the point of view is completely reversed. Practical
emphasis falls always not on this life, but on that which
awaits man on the other side of bodily death. It is *there*,
not *here*, that we are told to look for our real home and
our true destiny. While we are here, we are sojourners
in a strange land where we must not expect to see any
full satisfaction for our deepest interests in life; we are
no more to " inherit the promises " here than Abraham
was to do so while he roamed about among Canaanites
and Hittites. It is not the hereafter which is now thought
of as an impoverished survival or " carry-over " from the
fuller life of the present; the present is no more than a
" porch " leading to the real life which is yet to come;
it is, indeed, for all its brevity, of infinite importance, but
it is important mainly because it is the one way of
approach to what lies beyond, not on its own account.
It is a short time of education and testing, and on our
response to the testing depends, for each of us, a destiny
which is fixed and final. We must not, indeed, misunderstand this distinction between the *now* and the *hereafter*. Though we have to be " born again " into the life
which is eternal, as we had to be born into our temporal
life, we are not to suppose that we must wait for that

second birth until the hour of physical death; we must pass through the new birth while we are yet here, if we are ever to know it at all, and once " re-born into eternity ", we can even here enter, in a way, into the concerns and interests of the true and indestructible life; but, in the main, we do so by hope and anticipation, not by actual possession of our inheritance.

Further, it is of supreme importance that this inheritance is not one which comes to us, as a matter of course, from our having been born as men; it is not simply " going on and not to die ", as one of our own poets has miscalled it, but a life of a new quality, with new interests and purposes, and it is a " gift of God ". Our claim to it, so to say, is not like that of the heir on whom an estate has been entailed from his birth, but rather like that of a legatee under a " testament "; and this is one of the fundamental distinctions between genuinely Christian teaching and all the forms of " spiritualism ". With the " spiritualist " the first and all-important matter is our " survival ". Usually, in our own society, he also believes in God, but his interest in God, when all is said, is secondary and superficial; his theism is an annexe to the main building. With the Christian, on the other hand, the thought of God is the primary thing, and it is only because he is already so " sure of God ", that he can also feel assured that he will himself " survive ", and that the life to which he is destined has the quality which makes " survival " so supremely worth while. Wherever we find a thinker who puts human immortality in the first place, or tries to base his conviction of the reality and worth of the gift on any ground independent of the character of the Giver, we may be sure that we are dealing with one who is at best no more than half a Christian,

This great inversion of point of view characteristic of Christianity had naturally a history of preliminary preparation behind it; if a revelation is not to fail of its effect, the minds of its recipients need to be made ready for it. In this case there was actually a double preparation, within the Jewish community and in the wider Gentile world outside, and the contributions of the two preparations to the conception in which they were to be brought together are rather different. Among the Israelites, the first stage of the preparation was mainly a negative one; by their insistence on the exclusive worship of Yahweh, which, as we have said, belongs wholly to the living, the prophets had effectually ruined any lingering influence of the older concern with " ghosts " and " deities of the underworld ". Such superstitions as the people may at one time have had of this kind were dead, and the field was left clear for the development of a more ethical and spiritual faith, the belief in a future resurrection of the righteous to a " better " life (and sometimes, also, of the evil to a life which is the morally inevitable consequence of their choice of evil). This belief in resurrection, though it was persistently rejected by the Sadducean, or conservative, party who were concerned to keep religion strictly within the limits of the letter of the written law, was clearly general among the people at large well before the time of our Lord. Two characteristics of it call for special remark. It was thought of definitely not as a persistence of the soul after the dissolution of the body, but as a resurrection and re-animation of the body itself, and it is to be remembered that this conception has been adopted into Christianity, which makes the resurrection of the " flesh " one of the articles of its creed. This might look at first like the crude fancy of a grossly materialistic popular imagination, but, on reflection, we ought to see that there is more in it than that. Even in its crudest forms it embodies the sound thought that the life which is to be a worthy destiny for man must not be that of a part of our nature persisting after the destruction of the rest; it must be a life of the whole man, in which he is not less, but infinitely more, alive that he was before his decease. Also it is to be noted that in this belief, which is that of " the people ", and not of a little band of " intellectuals ", the link between our conduct here and now and our final destiny is thought of, not as it might have been by philosophers, as being that the second is the natural and necessary consequence of the first, but as established by the intervention of God, who " rewards " the righteous and " punishes " the wicked, in the manner of an earthly sovereign.

Here again, we have a thought which can be, and has been, abused with unhappy consequences; yet the central idea is fundamentally sound. The " reward " or " punishment ", however inadequately conceived (and the remains of Jewish and early Christian apocalypse show how gross the popular conceptions could be), is, from first to last, bestowed by God; what we have to hope or fear for ourselves is a consequence not of some vague impersonal " nature of things ", but of the character of the supreme personal Being of Beings; the final reward may be trusted to be wholly reasonable and right because it is " th' unsearchable dispose Of highest *wisdom* ". One might say, perhaps, that while the conception of eternal life revealed by Jewish apocalyptic is commonly at fault in representing the quality of such a life too much in terms of that which we know, it is entirely sound in thinking of it as a life of the whole man and in connecting it directly and intimately with the idea of God,

The preparation in the Gentile world is due primarily to the Platonic philosophy. Here, too, the break with "primitive superstition" is complete; Plato has to pave the way for his own conception by first dismissing with contempt the whole crew of goblins and ghosts which haunt the popular imagination. And when we come to his own convictions, we find that in one respect they are more adequate than those of the mass of Jewish believers in the "resurrection". He is emphatic on the matter of the *quality* of the immortality which he teaches. It is a life which has the centre of all its interests in the things which are not seen, and therefore commonly go unregarded: truth, goodness, beauty. If a man is to enter upon it, his whole outlook in the world must be reversed: "the soil must be *turned about*" if the rays of the true light are to fall upon it; as we should say, there must be a *conversion*. Plato understood well enough what most of the writers of the apocalypses never fully took in, that "the Kingdom of God is not meat and drink, but *righteousness*, peace, and joy"; no paradise of feasting and wassail would ever have satisfied him, even though its streets might be of gold and its gates of pearls.

But Plato is weak just where the Israelite is strong. His "immortality" of the parted soul, in which the body has no share, is, after all, dangerously like a doctrine of the survival of half a personality. And we also miss in him an adequate sense of the direct dependence of the hope of eternal life on the moral character of God. He is confident enough that the very reason why the soul can withstand the crisis of death is that it is "godlike" in its nature, and that the good man is the man of all others who is most "like God"; he is eloquent enough in his insistence that the universal law by which every man reaps the destiny he has earned is the appointment

of God. But when he offers reasons for the faith that is
in him, his justification of his assurance of immortality
is found altogether in consideration not of the character
of God, but the inherent nature of the soul, and it is
left an obscure point in his teaching what the relation of
our souls to God is, whether they do not, after all, exist
and exist deathlessly in their own right. And the consequence is that with all Plato's sincere belief in God's
judgment of men according to their works, he leaves it
to be supposed that the righteous man, in the end, wins
the crown by his own unaided effort. God has so ordered
the world that if he lives rightly he will achieve salvation,
but there is no *grace*, no " free gift " of God to enable
him to do so. God is, so to say, like a kindly and upright
judge in an athletic contest: He likes to see a competitor
do his best bravely and manfully, and will crown him
if he comes out successfully, but He does not and must
not intervene to help in his struggle. It was left for
Christianity to integrate in one conception the thoughts
of the newer and higher quality of the " immortal " life,
and those of God as its only source and guarantee, and
of the preservation of the whole man, not merely of a
favoured element in him " unto everlasting life ". What
we have to ask ourselves is whether the resulting Christian conception is coherent in itself, and whether it can
hold its own in the face of all our added knowledge of
the natural world and man as a member of it. In raising
these questions and trying to answer them, the appeal
will be made simply to our common rationality; there
will be no invoking of the ultra-rational authority either
of Church or of Scripture. The question is whether the
very foundations of the Christian view of life are tenable,
and in dealing with such a question we manifestly cannot
take one part of the Christian scheme for granted to

prove another. And it must be remembered that the writer claims no more than to be sincerely expressing his own mind according to his lights; he does not profess anywhere to speak the official sentiments of any church, sect, or party.

II

Suppose, then, that we make a beginning by asking ourselves the question whether, as intelligent men, we can believe at all in a life which is not destroyed by the dissolution of the body. Are there insuperable difficulties in the way of any such belief, and if there are not, are there any positive reasons, weak or strong, for believing? May we believe at all, and if we may, is there any reason why we should? I think we may at least say at once that there are clearly no sufficient reasons for simply refusing to entertain the belief. The alleged proofs of its absurdity amount only to this, that we know (or at least believe with full conviction) that we all have to die, and that when a man has once died we have no evidence that he is anything any longer. For all that we can tell he may simply have ceased to be. Now this "argument" is clearly worthless, and should really be left to "free thinkers" who are only half-wits. All that it really proves is something which Christianity would never dream of denying, namely, that at death a man's existence as an animate and intelligent person ceases to be certifiable for the surviving observers (at least unless we are willing to admit the reality of the comparatively rare and always disputable cases of "apparitions of the deceased"). Our friend who has died will no longer be seen and heard among us, even his inanimate body, which for a time we can still observe, will sooner or later fall to pieces and, in the main, be resolved into imperceptible constituents. The living man, then, by dying has ceased to be what he was before, an object accessible to our perception.

But this is no proof whatever that he has simply ceased to be. The mere fact that something has become imperceptible is no proof that it has become non-existent. And the fact that the deceased person is no longer a recognizable object for us is no proof that he is not still a very real object indeed for intelligences (if there are such intelligences, and we have no right to assume that there are not), who are not cramped by the narrow limits set by our organs of sensibility to the range of our perceptions. We are never safe in declaring that anything which our senses cannot detect must be nothing at all.

And in the case of a conscious self or a person there is a further consideration to be taken into account. The very word " existence " as applied to a *person* has a double sense. It may mean existence as one *object* among others perceptible by *other* persons as part of their " environment ". But it may also mean existence as a *subject* aware of itself, and it is not at all self-evident or demonstrable that these two senses, or modalities, of existence *must* always go together. We are not entitled to say, for example, that a person or self cannot be aware of itself without also being aware of objects which are not itself; there are even certain experiences which would suggest that this assertion would be false. We do sometimes seem to be aware of our own being, and of wellbeing or the contrary, without being aware of anything else. And equally it is by no means clear that I might not be fully aware of my own being, though no one else in the universe was aware of my presence as part of his " environment ". These are at least logical possibilities, and since they are logical possibilities, we should be careful to remember that, though we may all have seen others die, none of us has had the experience of dying in his own person. We know what kind of change occurs " objectively " in our environment when another dies; we do not know what the experienced change is to the *subject* who dies, and never shall know this until we die ourselves. (Even then we shall not know if to die is really to become nothing at all.) We have, then, no right to argue that the person who ceases to be capable of detection as an object going to make up our perceptible environment has ceased to be a *subject* with a continued experience of his own. For all that the ascertainable facts can tell us, he may literally simply have entered on " another life ".

But though this might be a sufficient rejoinder to mere confident dogmatism about the impossibility of life beyond death, it is not sufficient ground for entertaining any serious hopes. If we are to believe in anything it is not enough that the thing in question should not be a logical impossibility; we must have adequate positive grounds for our belief. We are thus led to ask where, if anywhere, such positive grounds for belief in life eternal and indestructible may be found. If we set aside for the present grounds directly borrowed from the experience of the religious life itself, we may say, I think, that warrant for the belief has commonly been sought along one or more of three lines: the appeal to certain alleged observable facts which are taken to prove the case, the appeal to a metaphysical theory of the nature of personality, or rational selfhood, the appeal to the character and requirements of the moral law. Some preliminary remarks may be made about each of these lines of argument.

As to the appeal (which covers the whole of the case for " survival " put forward by " spiritualists ") to certain alleged facts of an unusual kind which, it is said, may be made matter of actual exact observation under experimental conditions, it is certainly wise to keep an open mind in dealing with such supposed facts. It is certain, and is freely admitted by those who make most of the " evidence " of this kind, that in many cases the supposedly " supernormal facts " are only taken to be so because they have been observed and reported by persons who have had insufficient training in rigidly accurate observation and description of the observed, and again that, for reasons too patent to require stating, there is a constant tendency to fraud on the part of reputed possessors of " supernormal " powers of perception; the temptations to cheat are so strong and so subtle that the " percipient " himself may often be quite uncertain whether he has cheated or not. These are certainly reasons for treating all evidence of this kind with great circumspection, and perhaps for rejecting the great bulk of it, but they do not necessarily prove the whole of it to be worthless. Most of the " supernormal " or abnormal occurrences appealed to may be really only perfectly normal events ill-observed or ill-described; many of them may be produced by conscious or unconscious trickery; it does not follow that there are no genuine disturbing and perplexing facts, inexplicable by the simple assumptions of the complacent materialistic science of the nineteenth century; the " high-and-mighty " attitude of too many " scientific men ", who simply decline to examine the alleged facts at all, is not really creditable to their intelligence.

What does make this appeal to " spiritualistic phenomena " of little or no value for our purpose is that, even if we admitted the alleged " evidence " in bulk, it is at once ambiguous and, for us, irrelevant. It is ambiguous, since at the most all that it proves is that the exceptional experiences on which it relies admit of no explanation by currently recognized scientific laws. This, even if

completely made out, does not in the least show that
the rival "spiritist" explanation is sound; the true
explanation might be different from both. Even if it
could be sufficiently demonstrated that some of the
"phenomena" must be deliberately produced by agents
other than embodied human beings, it would not follow
that these agents are departed men and women. As
F. H. Bradley put it, the strongest conviction that can be
produced in this fashion takes the form "if that was not
my late brother's spirit, it must have been the devil",
and the second alternative is always possibly the right
one. If we grant the existence of normally invisible
selves who can, from time to time, intervene in the
course of affairs around us, we have no right to say that
all these agents must be deceased human beings; we
cannot simply refuse to face the possibility that they are
malevolent or mischievous non-human agents who contrive a masquerade of this kind for our delusion.

In any case the alleged evidence is irrelevant to the
Christian hope of the "better" life. It would be something to have apparent proof that the men who were
wise and virtuous while they were among us are wiser
and more virtuous now that they have left our company.
But what we really find is very different. Utterances
which profess to come from beings who were once
great poets or philosophers are doggerel or twaddle; the
preachments of the "spirits" of men who were great
moralists are sentimental puerilities. The life which
would be disclosed by such revelations, if we took
them seriously, would not be a life nearer to God, the
fountain of wisdom and goodness; it would rather be
one of intellectual and moral idiocy. I do not think it
too much to say of the most harmless of these "messages
from beyond the tomb" that, if they are what they

claim to be, we can only hope that the unseen world, like the seen, has its homes for the feeble-minded, and that it is with their inmates that our occultists are in communication.

More promising is the line of thought represented by Plato and so many of the great philosophers since Plato's day who have tried to prove by considerations of metaphysics that a self, or at any rate a rational self, a *person*, is, in its intrinsic nature indestructible, and being also in its intrinsic nature rational, can only be exposed to the dangers of intellectual and moral unreason temporarily and incidentally while the connection with a gross and corruptible body is maintained. This is the thought which at bottom inspires all the repeated attempts of philosophers to demonstrate the " natural immortality of the human soul ". One would never wish to speak without becoming respect of reasonings which have satisfied the minds of such men as Plato, St. Thomas Aquinas, and Leibniz. Yet it can hardly be doubted that the verdict of impartial reflection on all these arguments must be that while they are impressive, and in various degrees suggestive, they are all inconclusive.

For example, in reply to the particular argument which had the most extended and long continued vogue of them all, down to the time of Kant, the argument from the alleged absolute *simplicity* of the rational soul to its indissolubility and so to its indestructibility, it might manifestly be replied that it is by no means obvious that a personality is something absolutely simple; it may rather have a complexity of very high order; and even if its simplicity be granted, the reasoning, it might be said, points in the wrong direction; it is the complex, not the simple, which is most capable of adequate self-adjustment to great and varied changes in " environment "; the simpler the soul is conceived to be, the more likely is it to be at the mercy of variations in its surroundings. To the reasoning which finally commended itself to Plato, that " souls " are original creators of " motion ", not requiring, like other things, to be set moving from without, and therefore, since they depend only upon themselves for their motion, can never cease to " move ", and so to be alive, it might be answered, with at least an appearance of plausibility, that, to raise no further difficulties, it is at least certain that in the world of our daily experience the " motions " of the soul recurrently sink to the level of the all but complete unconsciousness of dreamless sleep or deep swoon; what then is to exclude the possibility that at death they sink permanently to a level of deeper unconsciousness still, and in that case, what kind of eternal life worth wasting a thought upon does the argument promise us? At most it can, by itself, do no more than suggest the bare possibility that death too is a profounder sleep from which there may be a waking, but suggestion is something very different from assurance. Or we may take the argument which is developed with such power at the end of the Platonic *Republic*, that nothing can be directly destroyed except by a " malady " or " evil " which is specific to its own nature (as, for example, a man must die of some derangement which is specifically a derangement of the animal organism, and poisonous food or air can only kill him indirectly by first inducing such a specific malady of his own nature). Now the one specific malady of the soul is " injustice " or wickedness; but we can easily see from experience that wickedness has, of itself, no tendency to destroy the self; the very wicked man in society is, in fact, often unusually mentally alert and alive. Since the one thing which is an intrinsic malady of the soul thus has no tendency to put an end to its existence, we may conclude that this existence is unending. Clearly the probative force of this reasoning depends on the assumption made all through that the " cause of a thing's dissolution " must always be looked for without and not within, and this assumption may at least be doubted until cogent justification has been offered for it.

There remains the practically widely influential moral argument for the life to come. Of this, too, a wise man would never speak without due respect. It is often misrepresented as though it was no more than a childish insistence that we shall get a certain thing merely because we very much wish to get it; we should very much like to go on living indefinitely, *ergo* we shall do so; we should all like a good time for ourselves and those of whom we approve, and to give a bad time to those whom we dislike or disapprove, and therefore, as we know that we cannot count on the fulfilment of these wishes in this life, there must be a world to come where they will be fulfilled. Hopes entertained with no better reason than this would certainly be perilous enough, but the real force of the moral argument cannot be judged by the caricatures of it put forward by the more unintelligent among unbelievers, not yet by the very unsatisfactory statements of it sometimes advanced by the more unintelligent among believers.

The real point of the argument can be better seen from a consideration of two characteristic utterances of two outstanding figures of the eighteenth century, Voltaire and Kant. In his well-known poem *On the Lisbon Earthquake* Voltaire is facing the moral problem suggested by the calamity: " Is there any sign in the order of nature that the source of that order is either intelligent

or morally righteous?" His answer is that the course of
the world's history appears to have no intelligible meaning at all, to say nothing of any moral significance—*if*
what we see of life is all that there is to see (a conclusion
in which he might have claimed to be treading in the
steps of St. Paul). But we do not know that it is all,
and so the last faltering word of the poem is that we
are not wholly bereft of *hope*. In Kant's *Critique of
Practical Reason* the wavering hope of Voltaire's poem has
become a sturdy *faith*. Kant's thought is that the unqualified and absolute reverence for the moral law which
is the inner spring of all genuinely moral action does not
permit the man of integrity to doubt that the law which
has this claim on the absolute reverence of every rational
being is the supreme law of the universe, no matter what
the appearances to the contrary. But the moral law
itself unconditionally demands from every one of us a
complete and utter conformity to itself, an inward holiness, which no man achieves in his life on earth; it also
imperatively demands that in the end a man shall be
happy—that is, his will shall take real effect—only in
proportion as it deserves to do so by its conformity to
moral law. If we absolutely reverence the moral law,
then, we must believe that there is an endless future
before us in which we can make unending advance to
complete holiness of will, and that the course of nature
is under the sovereignty of a moral and all-wise reader
of hearts who will so shape it that the deserved " happiness ", which the good man cannot directly seek after
without degrading duty into a means to an ulterior end,
shall come to him unsought in the degree to which he
deserves it, and because he deserves it.

The question is thus not one about what we should
like to have; probably most of us would by no means like

to have a "happiness" sternly proportioned to the single-mindedness of our devotion to duty for its own sake. For which of us is thus devoted to duty as he knows he ought to be? The thought is rather that if the scheme of things is a reasonable scheme at all, and not a nightmare, it must realize a purpose, and that purpose must be one of which, *if* we could have it set before us, as we cannot while we are still actors in the temporal drama, intelligence and conscience would approve. It is no proof that the scheme of things is irrational to say that I, with my circumscribed range of vision, do not see its justification, but to doubt that it *has* such a justification would be denying its rationality, the very presupposition on which science itself, no less than morality, is founded. And the denial cannot be escaped if the life we see is all the life there is.

Thus stated, the moral argument deserves all respect. It states no more than the demand every intelligent and virtuous person is entitled to make of the universe, if it is to approve itself to his reason and conscience. But if we treat it, as Kant proposed to do, as the one and only ground of hopes about our destiny, it discloses an obvious weakness. It tells us, indeed, what the universe must be if reason and conscience can approve of it, what the universe is, if it is true that moral law is supreme throughout it. But how do we know that the moral law is thus supreme? No one is clearer than Kant himself on the point that there can be no question of demonstration. We reverence the moral law unreservedly not because we can *prove* that it is entitled to this reverence, but because we should be already vicious at heart if we did not. After all, then, it may be said this reverence for the moral law may be no more than an illegitimate deification of rules and prohibitions of our own devising.

They may be as important as the moralist pleases for our parochial affairs on this planet, but with what shadow of right do we convert them into a legislation for the whole universe? If we have not the right to do this, has Kant any ground left for his faith? A universe of which the measure is given by what we see in this life would be unsatisfactory to reason and conscience. *Soit*; but what if the real universe *is* unsatisfactory, the product, as Hume put it, of an author who is childish or senile? Or, it may be, the work of no " author " at all? Clearly if we are to meet these objections, we cannot trust to the " moral argument " alone. It will have at least to be integrated with " metaphysical " considerations of what is implied in the very existence of an historical world, and perhaps also with considerations of a directly religious order. Otherwise we shall be attempting the impossible task of extracting information about that which is solely from premises which deal with what ought to be.

III

OUR preliminary results, so far, have been in the main negative. We have urged that even the bare fact of survival of death (to say nothing of the hope of a new quality of life) cannot be unambiguously established by the methods of experimental science; that arguments based on the assumed intrinsic nature of personality are inconclusive when taken by themselves; that the attempt to reach assurance by consideration of what is implied in the upright man's sense of the supreme reverence due to the moral law is equally indecisive unless we can also presuppose a " metaphysical " doctrine about the structure of the universe which clearly contains as an integral part of itself the very result we are trying to reach. We are thus driven to make a new beginning in our inquiry. We shall try, as impartially as we can, to ask ourselves what it means to be alive, and alive as a person who is capable of response both to the command of duty and to the solicitation to worship. It may be that when we take all the facts of our human situation fairly into account we shall find reason to entertain anticipations for ourselves and our fellows which are met adequately only by the specifically Christian conception of eternal life. If so, we shall have done all that can be expected of us, we shall have vindicated the reasonableness of faith in a " revelation ", a disclosure which, now that it has been made, is seen to satisfy the demands of the intelligence, though it was not reached, and could not have been reached, by any process of formal and abstract reasoning.

What, then, does it mean to be alive as a self at all? (I do not yet say, to be alive as a person, a reflective and thinking self.) As we have already said, to *exist* as a self does not mean simply to be there as one among a multitude of things which an observer must take account of in his attempt to describe what he finds before his notice and to shape his own actions accordingly. Existence in that sense must be ascribed to an indefinite multiplicity of things which cannot intelligibly be said to be living selves. The stone in my path exists as an object presented to my notice, for I shall trip, or stumble, or hurt myself, if I do not walk round it, or lift my foot to step over it. I exist, and my dog, if I have one, exists in that sense no less than the stone. You have to shape your path so as to avoid running into the dog, or into me, as you have to avoid running against stocks or stones. But in the case of the stone, it is enough for you to avoid colliding with it; you may come to trouble with the dog, or with me, without any physical collision, if you " hurt our feelings ", or " arouse our hostility ". We, in a word, can *feel*, as the stone apparently cannot. That I can feel is a fact of which I need no evidence, an immediate fact of " consciousness " in the old Scottish sense of the word, and that my dog can feel is so certain that it has never been doubted except by Cartesian philosophers wedded to a theory for which the fact was a disconcerting one.

Now when I say that it is an immediately certain fact that I feel, I do not mean that I observe among the multitude of things presented to my notice one thing of a certain size, shape, and colour which exhibits certain eccentricities of behaviour; " reacting ", for example, to one " stimulus " by a tear or a frown, and to another by a caressing movement or a smile. All this is only as much as I might learn about you by observing you, but it never occurs to me to suppose that you are myself, or that I feel your experiences. I can, to a certain extent, observe my own behaviour, much as I do that of other selves and things, though it is hard to learn to do this accurately, and the attitude cannot be consistently maintained for long together. But the whole point of the statement that what is being thus observed is *myself* lies in something which is added to the observations, the *identification* of the particular " object " now under notice with that which is experiencing the observing, the " subject " which *has* the feelings, and this " subject " is precisely just the one thing in the universe which is not a " presented object " among others. It is not one of the things " found there ", but that which finds them, exactly as the eye is that which sees other things but does not see itself. (Or if you object that indirectly, by the use of a mirror, the eye can be made to see itself, the real point is left untouched; I may see my eye in the mirror, but I do not see its *seeing* in the mirror any more than I see your seeing when I look into your eyes). The very possibility of the simplest experience is thus dependent on a mysterious act of identification, an identification of one of the " things observed " as in some way the same thing with that which " finds " all these things there without being one of them. Without this act of identification, no feeling and no selves.

Naturally and unavoidably in the last paragraph the appeal has been made to the reader's experience of *himself* as a " subject ", the only experience, in the strictest sense of the word, which he can have, and the reader's experience is that of one who is not merely a self but a person, a *thinking* self. We have no grounds to believe that the subhuman animals think or reflect, except in the most inchoate way and in exceptional moments; most of them, perhaps, never genuinely think at all. Yet it is plainly true that each of them feels, and so is something more than an object among others; each is an *experiencer* in its degree, not merely an object to be experienced. Each of them is a self, though a self of a lowly order, at once the feeler and the felt. Each, like ourselves, though in its own particular way, *possesses* the contents of its experience. The creature which can, in however rudimentary a way, "learn by experience" does not merely behave differently for the outside observer when it has so learned, it is different for itself, it *feels* differently. This means that the distinction between what a thing *appears* to be and what it *is* comes to have, in the case of all such creatures, a significance it has not in reference to anything inanimate. In reference to an inanimate thing this distinction between what it appears to be and what it is is only a distinction between what is observed by an inaccurate or hasty onlooker, and what is observed, or observable, by one who is more accurate and careful. In the case of the self which feels there is the much more important distinction between the creature as it can be observed and described from without by the most careful and thorough of observers, and the same creature as it is directly for itself, as the centre of a unique and incommunicable experiencing. Every self has this strictly incommunicable and hidden existence of its own as the *subject* of its experiences, that which *has* them all, but is itself none of them. This was why we remarked in an earlier paragraph that the vital question about what happens at death is not what dying looks like to the outside observer—a question easy enough to answer in principle—but what the experience of dying is to the self who is experiencing it. What is it to experience dying?

Now this question at once raises a grave difficulty.

Can dying ever be experienced at all? If to die means not merely to cease to be among the objects which make up the field of some other self's observation, but to cease to be a subject experiencing anything, to experience dying should mean to experience the transition from having experiences to having none, from feeling to feeling nothing. But to experience the total absence of experience, to feel that one is feeling nothing, is surely a contradiction in set terms, and unless both conditions are experienced, there can be no experience of the passage from the one to the other. It should seem then that dying, if it means the cessation of existence as an experiencing subject, must be an event which no creature can ever experience, just as none can experience the event of coming into being, in the sense of transition from being nothing at all to being something. Both, if they occur, are events in their own nature of such a kind that they can never be experienced by anyone, but at most, observed by those who are not experiencing them. And *their* observations, as we said, cannot be conclusive. The observer can satisfy himself that something is now perceptible which was formerly imperceptible, or something formerly perceptible now imperceptible; he cannot actually observe non-existence passing into existence, or existence into non-existence. Both transitions, if they occur, are as incapable of being observed as they are of being experienced. And the reason why they are incapable of being observed is not simply that, like physical events which are asserted to take place in the sub-microscopic world, they are on too small a scale for us to detect them, or that, in some further way, the physical conditions necessary for the stimulation of our sense-organs are not fulfilled; it is that it is a formal logical absurdity to think of a condition of non-existence at all;

there is no such condition, and therefore there can be no transition from it to anything else, or from anything else to it. The coming to be of something before wholly non-existent would be no transformation or transition, but absolute *origination*, and the sheer ceasing of anything existent to be would be *annihilation*.

Men of science, who concern themselves exclusively with " nature ", the field of " things presented to our observation ", simply presupposing (as for their purpose they are fully entitled to do) the observer of the field as a datum with which they are not concerned, are, of course, quite alive to the fact. They never, as students of science, deal with absolute beginnings or absolute endings. Even when they talk, as they are doing to some extent to-day, of a " creation " of the world, or of an end of the world, their language shows clearly enough that they do not mean an absolute beginning or ending. " Creation " with them, unless they supplement their science by an appeal to their personal theological convictions, means no more than the transition of something already in existence into a new form in which it becomes amenable to their scientific formulae, and annihilation no more than transition to a state in which the formulae are no longer applicable. Hence Sir James Jeans, for example, can talk freely of the *annihilation* of " matter " when he means simply the conversion of mass into " energy of radiation " (whatever that may be), and is so far from believing in any real annihilation that he can assume that, in this conversion, a definite amount of the one is replaced by a definite amount of the other.

It is still more difficult to think of an absolute beginning or cessation of selfhood, or subjecthood. We may try to imagine experiencing, consciousness, as somehow arising, at a certain stage, in history in a world from which it had been wholly absent. But this would be the same thing as to imagine that what had hitherto existed only as a thing possibly to be noticed by an outside observer had suddenly become itself the observer of itself and other things; that transition seems as unthinkable as it is unthinkable that reflections in a mirror should turn into beings who might see themselves, and us. A field of presented objects *presupposes* an actual or possible observer, who is not one of them; it does not account for him. We must therefore dismiss all attempts to think of the " emergence " of consciousness in a universe from which it was originally absent. *Experiencing*, awareness, of some sort must be at least coeval with the world of objects. (It may, indeed, be more than merely coeval with the world, since, as we have said, there seem to be some experiences—like those in which consciousness is filled with the sense of pleasure or pain—which are not awareness of objects but simply the experiencer's possession of his *own* being.)

As for particular owners of experience, like you and me, this leaves it still an open question whether or not we must think of ourselves as having a first origination or final annihilation. If we have, we can, of course, experience neither, since no one can experience being without experience, nor yet can the observations of others tell us anything conclusive on such a matter. But supposing what we have just been saying to be sound, it will follow that our first beginning and our final ending, if we have any, cannot be the effects of mere change in the " natural " world of presented objects. Either we must sit down content with the assertion that selves begin to be and cease to be without any reason at all, or we must look for the reasons for this beginning and ending (assuming them to be really facts) in creative or annihilating activity on the part of a being which is itself a primary self (or subject), standing outside and above all the vicissitudes of birth and death. It was thus not without reason that " early man " seems universally to have taken it for granted that the dead have not passed from existence to non-entity, but from one state of existence to another. And we can understand how Leibniz, the most extraordinary man of genius of modern times, could insist in his philosophy on asserting the immortality, not merely of " the soul ", but of " the animal ".

IV

Bᵁᵀ a human self is not merely a self like that of a dog or cat; it is something more, a *personal* self; we cannot, if we are to think reasonably about its origin and destiny, omit to consider what this personality may imply. What, then, are we asserting when we say that a man has personality, or is a person? We shall not do amiss in discussing the question to start from the famous definition given by Boethius, more than fourteen hundred years ago, in a sentence which sums up the results of more than a millenium of Græco-Roman philosophical thinking, and becomes a starting-point for the whole development of subsequent Christian theology and philosophy: *A person is an individual substance of rational nature.* A person, that is, is on the one hand unitary, is *a* self, or *one* self—unlike, for example, a swarm of bees, a flock of sheep, or a concourse, or tribe, or nation of men. The swarm or flock is made up of selves, the tribe or nation is made up of persons, but the swarm or flock is not actually a self, or the nation or tribe a person, and when we speak of them as though the one were a self, or the other a person, as we often enough do, we are using a metaphor which may easily mislead us if we once forget that it is only a metaphor. The flock or the nation may be said to have experiences, but it only has them because the individual sheep or men of which it is composed have them, and it has no experiences which are not those of some or other of its component sheep or men; it is not itself a centre of further experiences. Or, to put it another way, the experiences we ascribe to

34

it only belong to it because they belong of first right to this or that constituent of it. But *this* sheep, or *this* man, owns its or his experiences of first right; they are not *its* possession on the strength of being first the possession of sub-constituents of it. When, for example, a whole flock or herd is said to see or hear something, or to feel hunger or thirst, this can only be said because all, or most, of the members of it see or hear, or feel hungry or thirsty; but a man is not said to see because his eyes see, or to hear because his ears hear, or to feel thirst because his throat and palate feel it. As Plato long ago remarked, it is not the eye which sees or the ear which hears, but the *man* who sees with his eyes and hears with his ears. Scatter the flock or disperse the tribe, and there will be still as much seeing and hearing and feeling as before; resolve the individual animal or man into con-stituents of any kind, and seeing, hearing and all the characteristic experiences of sheep or man are abolished. The man or the animal is one in a special way in which no group or combination of men or animals is one.

But on the other hand, a person is an individual of a *rational* nature, not a mere self, but a reasonable or intelligent self. The person can not merely feel, but think and reflect; he not only owns his experiences, but is aware that he owns them. To be a person, or reasonable self, is not merely to possess one's own being, but to know that one possesses it; only when we have reached that knowledge are we capable of saying *I*, and he who cannot say to himself " *I am* " is not yet a person. We see this interestingly illustrated in the utterances of young children. A very young child will often speak of himself " in the third person ", by the name he hears applied to him by those around him, before he has learned to say *I*; he will say, " Jacky (or Tommy) wants this or that " before he says " *I* want it." Here we have a being who already is an experiencing subject or self —if he were not, he could feel no wants—and is also interested in an object in the field of his observation which he will one day discover to be in a unique way identical with the experiencer observing it, but he has not yet made the identification; when it has been made, he will no longer talk of what Jacky (or Tommy) wants, but of what " I want ". I have known the still more interesting case of a child who, as far as could be discovered (and I watched him carefully) never thus spoke of himself " in the third person "; until he learned to say *I*, he always spoke of himself as *you*. He had apparently discovered, by the time he began to speak at all, that the particular object which stood out so prominently in the field of his interests and observations was more than a " presented object ", was, in fact, a *self*, but not that it was his self. He had learned the difference between a person and a thing before he had come to knowledge of his *own* personality.

This discovery of our own personality has a double significance: it is the source of what Kant calls the *practical* and what he calls the *speculative* use of reason; the possibility both of morality and of science depends upon it. On the one hand, the being who has come to know himself as a person and by the same process to recognize those around him as persons like himself, is now in a position to think of himself as having reasonable and rightful expectations in respect of the treatment he receives from the other persons, and of them similarly as having rightful and reasonable claims in respect of the treatment they get from him, and here we have the simple beginnings of all that will subsequently expand into a whole code of moral rights and duties. Kant's famous attempt to reduce the whole content of morality to the principle that every man's personality is always to be treated by every man with unqualified reverence may not be entirely successful, since there are some duties (like that of humanity to the lower animals) which it cannot perhaps fairly be made to cover. But it is at least true that genuine morality only becomes possible in principle when we recognize that a person is always to be treated as a person, never as a mere animal self, and still less as a thing with no selfhood at all. And our morality is still implicit rather than explicit until we understand that this right of a person to be treated as personal belongs to him *as* a person, not as one connected with ourselves by the further bond of kindred, or race, or nationality, or friendship. There are *no* " lesser breeds without the law ", if that means " breeds " towards which we are discharged from its obligations. In this way the discovery of our own personality is the beginning of morality (the *practical* use of reason).

Again, it is when he has discovered his own personality that man ceases to take events as they happen to come and go, with the incurious acquiescence of the animals. He now feels that he has a right to ask *why* they come and go thus and not otherwise, the right of an intelligent being to an intelligible answer to his demand for the why and wherefore of things; and it is here that the speculative employment of reason from which the sciences are born takes its rise. Men are not merely intrigued and inquisitive, as some of the higher animals also are, about the novel and unfamiliar: with these animals curiosity often enough ends in the pulling of the unfamiliar thing to pieces, but it does not lead even to the rudiments of science. A man's curiosity has the further characteristic of being *intelligent* curiosity which will be contented with nothing short of what he can accept as a coherent and *reasonable* account of the " why and wherefore ". He goes on the tacit assumption that there is an intrinsic reasonableness of pattern in the world of " objects ", answering to the intelligence he finds in himself as the experiencing " subject ". (Of course at a stage at which his own intelligence is still undeveloped, what appears to him an intelligible connection is very often one which our more developed intelligence pronounces unintelligible, but that is another matter.) He expects of the course of events that it shall be an intelligible pattern, as he expects intelligible pattern in the connection of his own actions, or those of other men, and science is born from this expectation—its success, so far as it goes, is the justification of the expectation—or else it is a mere inexplicable " lucky accident "

And there is still a further point to note. Rational selfhood, intelligent personality, in ourselves is something which has to be gradually won, and that not without difficulty; we inherit it only in part and with many fluctuations of degree, and *prima facie* it goes as it comes. In what we see of the life of children, or remember of our own childhood, we seem to see a self which at first cannot be discriminated by observation from that of a mere *feeling* being growing by degrees into that of the *thinking* person, as we gradually bring more and more of steady conscious purpose into the control of our own actions, and discover more and more of coherent pattern in the sequence of events round us. The process is never finally completed; there are tracts of our experience (notably, for example, our dreams) in which moral principle and " patternedness " of sequence seem to be alike in abeyance; even in waking life, the man who has, in his prime, apparently attained high success in the moral ordering of his own life and the coherent understanding of the pattern of events often seems to relapse into moral and intellectual " childishness " if his days are sufficiently prolonged. Complete personality, then—the self's full and conscious possession of itself and its " environment "—would seem, in the world of our experience, to be always an unattained ideal; all science and all morality consist in the approach to it, but not in the possession of it. To *be* a full and complete person would be at once to have a plan and purpose in one's own life subject to no anterior vacillation and disturbance and to understand the whole world in a way which left nothing in it baffling and unintelligible. To such a being defeat and death would have lost all its meaning; his life would be strictly *eternal* life.

This train of reflection at once suggests to us several things. In the first place, it is no more possible to think of personality, rational selfhood, as " emerging on the scene as a product of evolution " than it is to think in the same way of selfhood itself. If we found it incredible that mere " experienced objects " should, of themselves, turn into " subjects of experience ", beings who can feel it is equally unthinkable that beings who can merely feel should, of themselves, turn into beings who can think and know. Personality, thinking and reasonable selfhood, must be no less irreducible to mere selfhood than selfhood is irreducible to thinghood. That is, there must be primitive and unoriginated personality, as well as primitive selfhood, at the very foundation of things. Our own imperfectly attained personality, always exposed to the dangers of lapse from its highest level, must be communicated from the unoriginated personality which knows " no variableness, neither shadow of turning ". Even if we had reason to think that our personal existence had no beginning in time, we should still have to regard it, because of its "variableness", as a *created* personality, depending for its being on the supreme uncreated personality. And this is not all. If uncreated complete personality is an irreducible fact, to such a personality there can be nothing in the universe which is unintelligible or not understood. All that is, or was, or will be must be transparent to the "eyes of Him with whom we have to do". But if this is so, then the whole world of being and all that it contains can have no source but Himself. If there could be anything which had its source elsewhere, there would be at once the possibility that "here is a thing which is unintelligible, not only to me, but to Him." The world itself must be His creation, an expression of His intelligence, intelligible through and through *because* its Author is pure and perfect intelligence.

Now to say as much as this implies more than might appear at first sight. A creation which is intelligible through and through because its Creator is pure and perfect intelligence must be intelligible not merely in the sense that some sort of pattern can be detected running through it—that much is true even of the mere play of a child—but in the deeper sense that the pattern so embodied is one which approves itself to a perfect intelligence as wholly and absolutely "worth while". There must be "meaning" in its structure and history in the same sense in which there is meaning in the great works of art which are the crowning glory of our human intelligence; whereas the artistically crude and bad is "unmeaning". The history of such a world must embody a purpose, and a purpose which, in the eyes of the perfectly intelligent Creator, is wholly and utterly good. In simpler words, a completely intelligible universe must also be a *moral* system, an embodiment of the great principles of *moral* value. There must be a moral purpose in the world's history, and the moral purpose must be universally good, if the world is really intelligible. This does not mean, of course, that we, with our imperfect insight and limited acquaintance with the course of history, must be able to see that the purpose is there, or how it is attained. To us, with our very imperfect knowledge of the facts of the past and the present, and our all but total ignorance of the future, the world may look to be a scene of moral confusion. Still less is it meant, as is too often assumed, that if there is a moral purpose in history, that purpose can only be to " make us all happy ". Even in our condition of imperfect knowledge of the course of fact, we can at least see for ourselves that the mere purpose of making all of us happy, irrespective of our conduct and characters, would hardly be one to commend itself to the perfect intelligence. We cannot, if we are serious men, well dispute Kant's dictum that the purpose to train us into making ourselves persons who *deserve* to be happy by the steady exercise of an intelligent and moral will is much more " worthy of " a perfectly intelligent and good Creator than the mere purpose to make us happy at all costs. It is true that we cannot directly *see* in the little we actually know of the world's history that this purpose is in fact attained, but at least we must *believe*, if we really believe that the world is intelligible, that if we could see the whole history of ourselves and our world " as God sees it ", we *should* find that, in spite of appearances, this purpose is attained. If it is not, the universe is in the end more or less irrational and unintelligible, and to make that admission is as fatal to science as it can be to morality.

Granted then that the history of the universe has a

purpose, and an intelligent moral purpose, it fairly follows that the course of that history treats a *person* as having the intrinsic and absolute right to respect, the moral value which morality declares to be inherent in him. A world in which beings having the conscious ideal of intelligent and moral personality before them, and so capable of being educated into such personality, only made their appearance to vanish again into impersonality would be as truly an irrational and unintelligible world as one in which the law of contradiction or the laws of arithmetic did not hold good. Either would be, quite literally, a " mad world ". But if the real world which is " the home of all of us " is intelligible, because the creature of an intelligent Creator, it is not a mad world but a sane one. We may reasonably believe, then, that it is what Keats called it, a " vale of soul-making ", and that it really provides for each of us the opportunity, if we will avail ourselves of it, of achieving the ideal which morality sets before us, growth into a full and complete personality in conscious possession of itself and all that ministers to it, no longer subject to disruptive influences from its own unexplored " consciousness ", or from a hostile " environment ". The real world, that is, provides for all of us the opportunity of attaining " eternal " life. So much, though no more, seems to me clearly implied in principle when we commit ourselves to the primary act of faith in rationality which is made by the simplest distinctions between *true* and *false*, *right* and *wrong*. If we are unwilling to make this act of faith, we should in consistency abstain from so much as asking a single question about the course of events or the path either of duty or of prudence, since we no longer have the right to regard one answer to such a question as more or less true than any other.

(It is not, of course, meant by speaking thus of faith in reason to encourage any spirit of hasty and superficial dogmatism. A sane man knows well enough that there are an infinity of questions which he cannot expect to decide confidently by a simple appeal to " his reason ". The facts which are needed as a basis for decision may be unascertainable to him; even when they are ascertainable, he knows only too well how unreasonable what he calls " his own reason " can be, how often he overlooks some fundamental link in the " chain of reasoning ", or takes for granted as " evident " something which is not evident, and is perhaps actually false. What he is really putting his faith in is not " his " reason, but the " reasonableness of things ", which, we have argued, implies the reality of a perfect reason which is not his own. His confidence is simply that the whole universe, natural and moral, is such that to a definite and intelligible question there is a definite and intelligible answer, though it may often enough be an answer which it is not, and never may be, in his power to give.)

So far we have been concerned with an attempt to indicate the state of mind in which a thoughtful and dispassionate inquirer, with an intelligent eye for all the relevant facts and no *parti pris*, would approach the specifically Christian teaching about the hope which " remains for the people of God ". He could come to the examination, if we are not mistaken, with a hope of his own for a life to come of a certain quality, a hope based ultimately on certain convictions (call them philosophical, or religious, or both, as you please) about the existence and nature of the Creator. The question for him would be whether the more specific anticipations of Christianity harmonize or conflict with these " anticipations of reason ". That issue we are now to consider, always, of course, remembering that the specific assertions of Christianity are made as matter of faith, and that there is no question of *demonstrating* their truth.

V

L ET us begin our examination, then, by setting down briefly some of the leading characteristics that seemed to us to distinguish an "immortality" such as it is reasonable at least to hope for from one which would be a mere arbitrary fancy without any rational justification.

(1) It is the attainment of a completed rational self-hood, or personality, conscious of itself and in harmonious possession both of all its own internal resources and of its "environment". Since it is only in and through intercourse with one another that personality is developed and maintained in us, such a life can only be that of a *society* of persons of one heart and mind from which the veil of mystery now making each of us so much a riddle to the rest, and the self-centred "private interest" which sets barriers to community of will, purpose, and sympathy have been eliminated.

(2) It is a life communicated to those who share in it, in the first instance, from the supreme personality pre-supposed by the very existence of the world and of ourselves. At that fountain our personality is fed; if we enter into and share the life of one another, in the way proper to moral persons, it is because we are all admitted to be sharers in His life. The "brotherhood of all men", so often dreamed of and longed for, is only possible in so far as all men recognize themselves as "sons of God".

(3) It is no privilege reserved to an *élite* of the richly dowered and gifted, but a heritage open to all mankind, high and low, learned and unlearned, refined or homely,

bond or free, in virtue of their common endowment with
the capacity for personality.

(4) But, though it is thus, in the end, an inheritance
and a gift, it is a gift which has to be appropriated by
genuine effort on our own part. We can render ourselves increasingly fit for it by steady and strenuous
endeavour, or we can fail more and more to appropriate
it by our own carelessness and sloth. Even in what we
now see of human life, we are familiar enough with the
fact that as a man uses or abuses his opportunities, he
tends to grow more and more into true personality or to
degenerate from it. It is possible to " save one's soul ",
but equally possible to lose it; eternal life can be won, but
it can also be thrown away. And thus, in the end, we
must expect it to be with each of us strictly " according
to his works ", good or evil, though we must never
allow ourselves to forget that it is only the supreme
Wisdom which knows the full good and evil of any man's
" work " as it truly is; the account is not to be rendered
to me, and my judgment of the quality of any man's
work, and particularly perhaps of that of my own, must
always be uncertain. To judge you or myself with the
judgment of God, I should need first to see myself or
you with the " all-seeing " eyes of the reader of all
hearts, and that vision is not vouchsafed to us in our
earthly pilgrimage.

(It should hardly be necessary, though to obviate a
certain kind of criticism it may be judicious to say that
in speaking of the Christian representation of the life
to come, our attention will be confined to the few and
reticent statements definitely made in the New Testament. We are not in the least concerned with the sometimes rather grotesque pictorial imagery of certain types
of popular hymn or sermon. Such utterances are no

part of the authoritative teaching of the Christian Church; their language, as everyone understands, is purely metaphorical, and the metaphors employed, being so largely borrowed from Old Testament poetry, are often not those which would spontaneously commend themselves to a modern European imagination, not to add that many of them have the further glaring fault of improperly transferring to the eternal life of " blessed spirits " in Heaven language used in the Apocalypse expressly of the " new Jerusalem " of an earthly " millennium ". The golden streets, gates of pearl and foundations of precious stones, for example, all belong to the seer's imaginative description of the renovated terrestrial city; they have nothing to do with " Heaven " and " eternity ".)

If we turn, then, to the four points we have just specified and take them in order, we shall, I believe, find that on each and all of them the teaching of Christianity exhibits a complete agreement with what we have called our natural and reasonable anticipations, but at the same time does more than merely repeat those anticipations; it adds something of its own, strictly in conformity with the " natural light ", but yet not discoverable apart from an actual historical disclosure, first through the " prophets ", and finally through the teaching, and even more, the life, death, and resurrection of our Lord Jesus Christ. Christianity—that is, if it is what it professes to be—is really a *revelation*, a disclosure of God's purposes for us, made from the side of God Himself, and, at the same time, the God to whom it bears witness is no other than the God to whom the careful and unbiased use of our own intelligence has been directing us. It is certainly a faith, but no less certainly, rightly apprehended a reasonable faith.

As to the first of our four points, we may note that the one thing definitely said about the hope held out to the Christian in the New Testament is that it is a being fully alive and fully conscious of the whole truth about our Maker, ourselves, and the world. Thus in the fourth Gospel the Evangelist's leading thought is that the divine Christ who, in the fullness of time has appeared among men, is Himself an eternal living personality, and has come into our midst in order to impart such personality to us. He was " in the beginning with God " and " was God ". All creation was made " through Him ", and, the writer goes on to explain—if we follow what seems the most probable punctuation—" that which was made was life in Him, and the life was the *light* of men ". The life, that is, which is eternally inherent in the Christ is no blind " life force "; it is an intelligent personality, like that we find in a most imperfect measure in ourselves at our best, and aspire to possess in a fuller manner. So in the great prayer of Chapter xvii. our Lord describes the eternal life, which it is His mission to bestow on those who believe, as consisting in knowledge of " the only true God and Jesus Christ whom He has sent ". What this implies is expressed in so many words in the First Epistle of John, where, amid all the reserve with which the writer confesses that we know and can know little or nothing, at present, of what eternal life is (" it doth not yet appear what we shall be "), he also insists that at least we shall be " like Him ", because " we shall see Him as He is ". That is, the knowledge of God as He is will transform us, as we attain to it, into God's likeness, since our personality inevitably shapes itself on the model of that which supplies the food of its habitual contemplation and meditation.

St. Paul again strikes the same note both in his reserves

and in his certainties. He, too, will commit himself to no rash theosophic dreams of the future which lies before him; as he tells his Corinthian converts " what God has prepared for them that love Him " is something which " has not entered into man's heart ", something transcending all our imaginative speculation; here on earth the best of us only see the reality dimly, through a mirror, so to say, and " in a riddle "; it is elsewhere, " yonder " as the Neo-Platonist philosophers were fond of saying, that it will be for us to see it as it is, and without the distortions which arise from the interposition of the " mirror ", to " know even as we are known ". Here our most certain knowledge is beset all around with a penumbra of obscurity and darkness; as the old proverb says, as soon as we pursue any of our inquiries more than a very little way, we come upon the inexplicable, *omnia abeunt in mysterium*; " yonder " there will be no unintelligibilities left, our vision will have the limpid transparency of God's, and our wills will be in perfect harmony with themselves and one another because our vision is clear. We shall be what we are here at best seeking to become, persons in full and conscious possession of our own personality.

The tradition of the great Christian divines has always been true to the lines thus laid down in the New Testament. The Greek Fathers did not shrink from translating the Johannine language about likeness to God as the result of " seeing Him as He is ", into the formula that the process of attaining eternal life is one of *theosis* (*deification*), becoming ourselves divine, and the formula was retained by the Western Church, though with a preference for replacing the word *deification*, which might be misunderstood as though it were meant to efface the impassable gulf between the Creator and His creatures,

by the less dangerous term, *deiformity*. If even that word
sounds too presumptuous to certain modern ears we may
gloss it by saying that in view of the thorough-going
rationalism of medieval Christian thought, to achieve
deiformity means neither more nor less than what we
have ourselves spoken of as the attainment of an assured
and conscious complete personality. When the great
men of the Middle Ages spoke of human life as a pilgrimage of the soul to God, they did not mean, as an
Indian Yogi might, that the goal of the pilgrim's journey
is to lose himself in the impersonal. "The dewdrops
slip into the boundless sea" may be a pretty phrase,
but to the Christian ear it is charged with deadly heresy;
the goal, as Christians have seen it, is not to lose one's
personal self, but to find it for the first time and to
find it beyond all possibility of loss. Certainly, according
to the Gospels, the man who is set on keeping a dwarfish
and misgrown self with its trivial lusts and limited and
conflicting loves, will in the end lose himself, but he who
is ready to set this more than half unreal self on the
hazard will end by finding himself "unto life eternal",
he will find the personality which God meant to be his,
and he is the only man who will do so.

As to our second point, it would be wasting words
to take up unnecessary space in dwelling on the fact
that eternal life is always represented in the New Testament as a *gift* from God. It is enough for us to remember that St. Paul lays special stress on the contrast between
the death which is the *wage* of sin and the eternal life
which is not a wage but a free gift of God, and that the
same thought reappears in the fourth Gospel when we
find Christ saying that He grants it to His disciples to
have life in themselves, as the Father has granted it to
Him to have life in Himself. It is more to our purpose

to note that the gift is not represented in the New Testament as bestowed on men by the fact of their creation. Men are not thought of as already sons of God and heirs of eternal life in virtue of their birth into the world as men; that is a modern " humanitarian " remodelling of the thought; according to the New Testament, men acquire sonship to God and the inheritance of eternal life by being " adopted " into the Christian fellowship; they are adopted, not natural sons of the Father in Heaven. This is why the first step on the way to eternal life can be called by St. Paul being a " *new* creation ", and in the fourth Gospel being " born *again* ", and why in the Epistle of St. Peter God is said to have " begotten us again unto a lively hope *by the resurrection of Jesus Christ* ". Those who are still outside the Christian fellowship are said, on the contrary, to be without hope in the world, and are spoken of not as sons of God, but as " children of wrath ". The Christian conception is that eternal life is a gift which Christ is empowered to confer on His followers, and only on them, though sight is never lost of the fact that any man is potentially a son of God, since any man may be re-born into the Christian fellowship.

This is not to say that the New Testament writers teach the doctrine of the " natural mortality of the soul ". As their constant references to judgment to come show, they accept as something familiar to themselves and their readers the belief that we all survive what we call the death of the body. It is possible, no doubt, by a suitable exegesis to read into their writings a doctrine of " conditional immortality ", if that phrase is taken to mean that the final doom of the man who distinctly rejects Christ and His gift is complete dissolution of personality, but we cannot force on them the thought this dissolution is effected at the death of the present body. That, they assume, we shall all survive. But such mere survival, even if indefinitely prolonged, is not what they mean by " incorruptibility " or eternal life. They keep those names for the new quality of life enjoyed by the man who is " with the Lord " and " sees Him as He is." This is a point which is unfortunately obscured when Christian thinkers set themselves, as they have often done in the past, to try to demonstrate the immortality of the soul by reasoning based simply on a theory of *its* nature, without any reference to God, except perhaps as the Creator of the soul and of everything else. It is therefore, perhaps, from the Christian point of view a gain that arguments of this kind have fallen under suspicion, even excessive suspicion, ever since Kant's vigorous onslaught on them in the *Critique of Pure Reason*. An " immortality " which could be demonstrated without any reference to God would be only an indefinite survival which might conceivably prove to be the fact in a world where there was no God at all; this is not the " better life " that any religiously minded man, least of all a Christian, is particularly interested in.

It should be hardly necessary to remark, again, that there is a complete absence from the New Testament of any trace of the insidious tendency to regard God's gift of a full and completed personality as restricted to some little aristocracy of the intellectually highly endowed. " Heaven ", as Christianity conceives it, is not reserved for " superior persons "; it is full of " common people ". This is, indeed, a direct consequence of the way in which, in the New Testament, the " promises " are regularly made not to the isolated individual, but to the whole society of the " re-born ". They are promises to a " you ", not to a " thou ". We can, of course, understand how, in the necessary reaction of modern times against the coarsening and hardening of the original thought of the Gospel into the notion of a " salvation " to be mechanically earned by membership of a particular visible organization, men's minds should have been driven in the opposite direction, to the point of regarding " religion " as a purely private affair between the individual soul and its God. But neither this extreme " protestantism " (which, of course, was never contemplated by the original Protestants) nor its opposite, an extreme " institutionalism " has any true warrant in the New Testament. According to the New Testament, " salvation " certainly depends on a *personal* relation between God and the individual soul; if a man has not in him " the spirit of Christ ", he is none of Christ's, no matter what he may seem to be from his superficial inclusion in any visible organization. But the personal relation is not a *private* one. It carries with it, and should normally show itself by, a relation of the most intimate kind to all the other persons who together constitute " the body of Christ ". Hence the inseparability of the love of God, which is the first commandment of the New Law from the love of one's neighbour, which is the second, and the apostle's insistence that absence of the love of the brethren may be taken as proof of the absence of love of God. This is, in fact, a consequence of the very nature of personality itself. Personality can only develop in an atmosphere of reciprocal intimate and loving fellowship between persons; the closer and more intimate this fellowship, the more real the personality attained by those who share in it; a narrow and " self-centred " person (even when, as may be often the case, his isolation is rather his misfortune than his fault) is not fully a person. St. Paul's way of putting this is to say that in virtue of the fact that each of us is a " member " of the body of Christ, we are also " members of one another ". Disease or weakness of one limb or organ of a living body inevitably has its effect on the health and strength of the whole, and the reason for the closeness of this connection between the different organs is precisely that all are related as " organs " to the life of the single self, which *is* not any of the " organs " but finds its expression through them all.

It is not meant that there is no distinction between the magnitude of the tasks executed by different organs; the very perfection of organization demands that there should be distinction and discrimination. But all alike, conspicuous or inconspicuous, primary or secondary, have their own special communication to make to the single life of the whole, and all are alike alive with its life. So in the Christian fellowship, not all who belong to it are apostles, or teachers, or share in the gifts of wisdom and knowledge to the same degree, but all are alike alive with the distinctive Christian life, all have in principle been " re-born into eternity ". In the community of the re-born there are no barriers of race, or colour, or class, and the degree to which any man has attained possession of *his* true personality is not to be measured by the place he holds in any scale drawn up with a view to mundane standards. A simple uninstructed man may rank much higher in the scale of genuine personality than a great scholar or man of science; an indigent negro than a " cultivated English gentleman ". Those of us whose work in the world is discharged in one of the so-called " learned professions ", perhaps, need particularly to be warned that whenever we yield to the temptation to confuse spiritual worth with intellectual attainments, or delicate taste, or " culture ", as the word is commonly understood, we are deserting the Christian standard.

Finally, though the eternal life spoken of in the New Testament is, in its origin, a free gift bestowed by God, it is one which has to be appropriated by the recipient, and the appropriation involves a lifetime of work and care. The gift may always be thrown away by our own wilfulness or carelessness, and none of us is secure against these faults. Hence the need that " he who seems to stand " should take unremitting care " lest he fall ". No New Testament writer is more emphatic in his declarations that eternal life is not a " wage " or " salary " for services rendered but a gift than St. Paul, but it is he also who most expressly enjoins his converts to " work out their own salvation " in " fear and trembling ", and openly envisages the possibility that, even in himself, negligence might end in " becoming a castaway ". The High Calvinists of a bygone age were accustomed to find the warrant for their assertion " once in grace, always in grace " in certain passages of the Epistle to the Romans; yet it is clear that the author of the epistle would never have ventured to say of himself what some of his exponents have said, that he *knew* himself to be now and for ever finally " in grace ".

If it is a paradox to say that something which is a free gift of God may also be forfeited unless we strive towards it diligently and unremittingly, it is a paradox which runs through the whole New Testament. No honest exegesis can get rid of the patent fact that, when all is said, the New Testament doctrine of man's destiny is no mere message of comfort for the indolent; there is a side to it which is distinctly disquieting. Eternal life can be won, and won by him who will, but it can also be thrown away, and apparently—though the New Testament, intelligently read, is not very explicit in this—finally thrown away. That any man has actually made such a final " great refusal " is, perhaps, more than the New Testament ever says, but at least, for each of us, there is the possibility of making it. It is emphatically *not* the Christian doctrine that the persistent " waster " has only to pass through the portals of death to find himself in a world which automatically " makes this world right ". And this also is as it should be if what is at stake is personality itself. Personality cannot be thrust upon us from without; it has to be asserted by each of us for himself by resolute concentration of thought and will, and if a man " lets himself drift ", he rapidly sinks to a more impersonal level. If I choose, I can degrade myself into something like a mere self of momentary impulses and feelings, and we all find that we are too apt to act thus, especially as age steals over us. We have no reason to suppose that it can be otherwise in the hereafter.

If what we have so far said is true, then, we may fairly claim for the Christian hope that, when rightly understood, it is no fantastic dream, pleasing but baseless; in substance it accords with anticipations which are independently inevitable in all of us, just because we are reasonable creatures in a universe where reason is at home. But Christianity also gives a new and determinate character to these anticipations, which would otherwise remain vague and uncertain, and because it does this, we rightly receive it as a " revelation ". It is wholly misleading to speak of Christianity, in the fashion of the eighteenth-century latitudinarians, as " the religion of nature republished ", with the implication that it contains only what might have been, and presumably was, equally well known to the reflective and devout of all ages, and that the mission of our Lord was no more than to remind the thoughtless of what they had allowed themselves to forget. Christ, according to the New Testament, did not come into the world simply to help men to " brush up " their " natural religion " as middle-aged men may " brush up " the French and Latin they learned in their schooldays. He came primarily not to *teach* us something in the short course of His earthly life, but to *do* something for us which no mere teacher could do; so far as He came to teach, it was to teach us something we did not know before, and without Him could not know at all.

What the New Testament adds to the statement that eternal life is the gift of God is, in the first place, that the gift has been bestowed on us specifically through Christ, and that Christ is no mere envoy through whom a far-away God has conveyed a message to us, but one who is Himself both a man of our own flesh and blood and also divine, " one with the Father ". (The New Testament writers do not, of course, use the technical terminology which was subsequently developed for the express purpose of putting an end to discussions about their meaning, but it is recognized to-day by scholars of all shades of personal opinion that the New Testament everywhere presents Christ as a divine being who may rightly receive the adoration due to God, and whose acts are rightly described as acts of God. It is just the impossibility of reducing the Lord Jesus of " primitive Christianity " to purely human dimensions which leads ingenious but ill-balanced writers in our own times to make attempts, discountenanced by all serious historians, Christian or non-Christian, to get rid altogether of the historical Jesus Christ and to reduce Him to a " myth ".

Preposterous [1] as the device is, it is prompted by the sound perception that the Christ of our earliest documents is *already* presented as a divine being.)

Now here is, as has been said—for example, by Dr. E. R. Bevan—the characteristically new note of the New Testament as compared with the Old. Ezekiel, in particular, had said long before that God would once more gather together his people, now scattered in bondage, as a shepherd might go out into the wilderness and collect his strayed flock. But to the Jewish reader this had apparently meant only that God would raise up in the future some wonderful human leader who would gather together again the " dispersion " of Israel. It would be, after all, only this wonderful man who could actually go out into the desert to reassemble the " sheep "; God would only be concerned in the business as the far-off being who had sent him on his costly and perilous errand, as a monarch may sit comfortably at home in his palace and send out devoted servants on a distant enterprise; the undertaking would be God's only on the principle that *qui facit per alium facit per se.* The courage and devotion would really be those of the envoy, and, to the strictly

[1] How preposterous is shown, for example, by the theory of some literary men that the Jesus of the Gospels is identical with the Joshua of the Old Testament. We are thus to assume (1) that Joshua was an old and forgotten Hebrew divinity, and (2) that at the Christian era there was, for some unknown reason, a revival of the cult of this obsolete god. But there is not one scrap of evidence that Joshua was ever regarded by any Israelite as being a deity. His story, as we have it in the Old Testament, is simply that of a successful leader of Hebrew tribes in their first penetration into the country of the Canaanites, and there is no reason to think that anyone had ever supposed him to be anything else. We do not even hear that the Israelites made a colossal statue of him and hammered nails into it for luck. The Germans did this sort of thing for Hindenburg some twenty years ago, but a man who should assert that Hindenburg was a resurrected Wotan would only make himself ridiculous.

logical mind, they would be proof of *his* goodness, but no proof of the goodness of the sovereign to whom they cost nothing. Christianity, on the other hand, declared that it was actual fact that the divine shepherd had Himself come into the wilderness after the strayed sheep and had faced all its hardships and privations in His own person. The historical events were thus witnesses to the self-forgetting love, not of a great teacher or prophet, but of the very Lord of creation Himself. " So God loved the world " thus came to have a depth of meaning for Christians which it had never had for an Israelite, and the new significance of the thought gave a new meaning to the Christian life as a response to this love; it was possible henceforth for life to be inspired by a supreme, grateful love, not simply to a great human benefactor, but to the Maker of " all things visible and invisible ".

The result is a changed attitude to the whole drama of human life and death. Even in a world morally indifferent—as the world depicted in Shakespeare's greatest tragedies sometimes looks to be—to good and bad; even in a world definitely and positively evil, we could still feel love and devotion to a human benefactor who had at least protected us, to the best of his power, against " fortune's spite "; some of us might steel ourselves, when he fell, to fall not utterly unmanned by his side. But in an evil world we should certainly know, and in an indifferent world we should have overpowering reasons for believing that our hero and we were at best falling together in a forlorn hope. The order of things would be against us, and our highest courage would be the courage of despair dying " game to the last ". Now despair can for a time nerve to vigorous achievement, but as a permanent attitude it is not invigorating but enervating. At least, it must be so with us, who are not

wolves or weasels but men, reasonable animals. If we are
once firmly convinced that the order of things is irre-
vocably against our ideals, we cannot avoid the paralyzing
suspicion that these ideals, however much we cherish
them, are futile and arbitrary, and we shall come to
ask ourselves doubtingly whether they are, after all,
worth the blood and tears they cost, whether mankind
had not better do without them.

This is why, for my own part, I doubt very much
whether a virile human morality can flourish apart from
some conviction about the universal world-order which,
thought out, proves to imply belief in God and His
goodness. One may say, no doubt, that " value " and
" existence " have nothing to do with one another, but
belong to wholly different worlds of thought; one may
say " What we need as inspiration to action is not belief
in the *existence* of any thing or any person, but belief in
the *worth* of courage and love ", and the like. But
divorced from belief in the overpowering actuality of the
" love whose smile kindles the universe ", your declara-
tion " I believe in love " only means " I personally
choose to regard love as supremely good "; and if your
only reason for your profession is a *Hoc volo, sic jubeo*,
why should you not change your choice? *Le peu de
chose que sont les hommes!* and if *l'amour* is, to put it
brutally, only an episode in the career of these little
creatures, *le peu de chose qu'est l'amour*.[1] It is, you will
say, what I care most about. But it is not what all men,
perhaps not what many men, care most about, and it
may be that to-morrow, or next year, I shall have

[1] Rupert Brooke wrote of the First World War as a welcome recall
from " all the little emptiness of love ". Presumably the kind of
" love " he had in his mind was none of the loftiest, but if the noblest
love we know is, after all, *only* the " idiosyncrasy " of a particular
species of animal, is it not all, in the end, " little " and " empty " ?

changed my scale of " values "; if these values are no more than creations of my personal will, there is nothing sacred about them, they arise and perish as my fancy flickers, like the " fancy values of commerce. There can, indeed, be no worth except in relation to some will which finds satisfaction in it, but the will to which genuine and abiding worth has this relation cannot be merely your mutable willing or mine; it can only be a " living will that shall endure when all that seems shall suffer shock ". To the good man love is sacred and duty is sacred, but neither could be so if they were mere expressions of his own will as this individual man; the good man is not an idolator of himself and his private will. And if I, or all mankind, were to-morrow to turn against the old sanctities and tread love and duty under our feet, they would lose nothing of their sacredness; it would not really be they, but our own wills, which would be profaned.

Now if the central doctrine of the Christian is true, then we have such a certainty as the world cannot otherwise afford that love and duty are indeed sacred. For then it is a fact that the Master of all things has not merely told us to be loving and dutiful and will hold us to account if we fail; He has Himself, in the person of the historical Lord Jesus, entered into the life of humanity, has Himself led the life of selfless love and duty to the bitter end, and triumphed over all the obstacles that beset it; we, who have still the obstacles and hindrances to conflict with, have received from him not merely the inspiration of His teaching and example, but the certainty that the values which are sustained by the eternal " living will " are precisely those which were affirmed in practice by the Lord Jesus and are dearest to our own hearts— love, dutifulness, humility, courage, patience. We know, then, that, however appearances may be against them, these values can "never fail"; they are the foundation-stones on which the frame of things is built. This is why an apostle can speak of the faith of the Christian fellowship as one which conquers the world. It is not merely that, to quote Blake, "a strong persuasion that a thing is so makes it so"; for you cannot make falsehood into truth by the violence of your "persuasion" of the falsehood. The "world-conquering" quality of the Christian faith, if it is not an illusion, depends, first and foremost, on the nature of the person towards whom it is directed. It can conquer the world because, if it is true at all, it is a confidence based on a real disclosure of the character of the unseen source of the world. If the mind of God has been truly disclosed by the life, death, and triumph of Jesus, then it is certain that God's world is not really either indifferent or hostile to our highest human aspirations, and for the true "members of Christ's body" eternal life ceases to be only what Plato had called it, a "great hope", and becomes a fact. It is the confidence in the fact which accounts for the strange "joy" so characteristic of the obscure, toil-worn, despised and persecuted first Christians in the midst of a world full of pleasures, refined or sordid, but, as students of the period have so often noted, as deficient in joy as it was avid of pleasure.

These considerations also explain what might otherwise seem a singular fact about the history of Christian theology. When the Church set itself to codify and formulate its convictions it was not content with the emphatic assertion of the divinity of its founder; it insisted no less emphatically on his genuine and complete humanity. If it was declared deadly heresy to pronounce him in any way "inferior to the Father as touching this divinity ", it was an equal heresy to abate anything from his humanity. You were not to withhold from him any jot of the worship due to the supreme Creator; equally you were not to exempt him from anything incidental to full human normality—hunger, thirst, weariness, pain, temptation. He was to be thought of neither as a deity of second rank, nor as a " superman ". This, more than anything else, was what perplexed and shocked the ordinary outsider. He would not have found it incredible that a god, at any rate a minor god, should show himself in the visible form of a man. But that a god should feel genuine want or pain, should shed tears at the grave of a friend, should be insulted, beaten, crucified, and should feel the pain and shame of such things was a veritable scandal. Yet obviously if the life of Christ is to be evidence that *our* highest human values are also the eternal and absolute values, it is precisely this union in one historical person of Deity and complete humanity which must be maintained. To whittle away either the divinity or the humanity—to be either " Liberal Protestant " or Docetist—is to surrender the very " ground of all our hopes ".

VI

IF what we have said about the specifically Christian hope of " life in the world to come" is in substance sound, we can safely draw certain distinctions between that hope and various imaginative speculations with which it is often confused. We need, in the first place, always to remember that the eternal life promised by Christianity is a *new* life into which the Christian is re-born by a direct contact between his own personality and the divine Spirit, not a prolongation of the " natural" life, with all its interests, into an indefinitely extended future. There must always be something " unworldly" in the Christian's hopes for his destiny after death, as there must be something unworldly in his present attitude to the life that now is. He is assured, if he perseveres, of the attainment of a true personality which will be a faithful " image" of the personality of the God in whom his affections have found their centre, and this must mean, at least, that he is sure of the retention of his genuine and real selfhood. There can be no question, for one who thinks as a Christian, of the merging of his personality into a vague and indifferentiated " ocean" of the divine; no literal " losing" of himself " in light". No " image" or " reflection", however faithful, is identical with that which is mirrored in it. It is essential to the Christian conception of God that, close as the creature may draw to the Creator in love and worship, there is also a great gulf fixed between them by the very fact that the one is Creator and the other creature, and that this gulf can never be spanned in time or eternity. " He is closer to

64

us ", as the Mohammedan phrase puts it, " than the vein of the neck," or as our own poet said, " than breathing ", and yet, with all the closeness, He remains for ever " absolutely *other* ". The saint in heaven lives on Him and from Him, as a man lives on the air he breathes; but he breathes with his own lungs, he lives with a life which is his *own* life, not his Creator's, and each several saint with a life which is his and not his fellow's.

But we must also remember that here in this world, where most of us have made so little progress in that winning of a true free personality which only comes by conquest over the rebellious element within ourselves, our notions of what the life of a free person would be are necessarily almost hopelessly vague. Such advance in the right direction as we may have made has always had to be made by receiving " impulses " to be better " in a wise passiveness ", but equally by actively detaching ourselves from the unworthy interests and false devotions which clog the spirit. And we never know how far further the detachment may have to be carried. It may be that to enter into eternal life any one of us would have to learn to detach himself from things which are still to him, in his natural human weakness, the very breath of life. If he could see his eternal future, as it is, it may be that he would shrink from it, that he is not yet ready to enter into it " with joy ", because the entrance would mean leaving behind so much without which, as it still seems to him, life would not be worth living. And we know, at least, that to all probability death must mean parting once and for all from the familiar things which their familiarity makes so wonderfully dear to us. Clearly, if Heaven is to be Heaven to a man, he must first have learned well and thoroughly the lesson " love not the world nor the things that are in the world . . . the world passeth away ". There is no one thing in " the world ", however good it may have been in its time and place, that a man must not be prepared to let go when the time comes, if it is eternal life on which his heart is set.

Nor is the austerity of this demand for detachment of spirit affected by the fact that, as we all know, Christianity has always insisted on including in the eternal life not merely, like Greek philosophy, the most precious part of a man, his " soul " or " mind ", but the whole man. There was, indeed, a very good reason for the Christian insistence on the " resurrection of the body ". The Christian's " world to come " is not one of solitary speculation, but one where the members love one another, are united in the " bond of charity "; and such a relation between persons who are irreducibly separate—for if they were not, they could not love one *another*—demands a " body " in the sense of a medium of intercommunication of thought and affection. But, as the Apostle was careful to say, that body is a " spiritual " one; we " shall all be changed ", and none of us knows, what that change may involve. The crude speculations of some medieval theologians about the " resurrection body " are really as incompatible with the apostolic reserve as they are with the known facts of modern science; and, I may add, they have never been at best more than the speculations of theologians they are not, and never have been, part of " the Faith ". For that it is sufficient that the eternal life, being a full personal life, must be thought of as a life of mutual intercourse between persons; for the rest, as to how this may be effected, we have no more than the information " God giveth it a body as it hath pleased Him ".

It follows that all attempts to depict to ourselves the

precise character of the life to come are mere fancies. There is not much harm done by these fancies when it is clearly understood that they are no more than imaginative pictures intended only to convey the thought that the saints are united in an adoring sense of the presence of God and brotherly love of one another and of their fellows still on earth. So understood, our imaginings are, no doubt, in their detail, " mythology ", but the kind of mythology of which any literature which rises above the bare level of a " chronicle " is made. Such mythology has a truth of its own, though not a literal truth. And even Christians often need to be reminded that the truth of such imaginations is not literal. There is a good deal of sentimental hymnology about Heaven which at least excuses Dr. Inge's comment that it is hard to know which would be the more dismal fate, to be everlastingly reciting encomiums or to be everlastingly listening to them. When our Lord said that the children of the resurrection would be " like the angels ", He did not mean that they would be long-winged creatures " with crowns upon their foreheads and harps within their hands ", but something very different, and not much in keeping with the tone of this vapid pietistic doggerel. Presumably the first readers of the Apocalypse of John the Divine, from which these descriptions are mainly drawn, would understand that his company of crowned harpers are figures as purely symbolic as his own four " beasts ", or the six-winged seraphim of Isaiah, and the cherubs of Ezekiel. But the symbolism is of a kind not familiar as symbolism to us in our ordinary reading, and probably modern Christian communities would do well to revise a good deal of their hymnology with an unsparing hand.

But if Christians have too often sunk into triviality in their pictures of the life eternal, there is something much worse to be said about a type of literature of which we probably all know something, the "mediumistic" descriptions of that life which profess to come from those who are actually leading it. Sometimes, indeed, these descriptions are only a little puerile, as when they represent the spirits of just men made perfect as spending eternity in a sort of picnic in a glorified "Lakeland". But often they are worse than trivial, they are sordid. We are expected to believe that the heroic dead derive their happiness from the consumption of spectral whiskies-and-sodas and the smoking of ghostly cigars, things which no intelligent man would reckon as more than very minor "conveniences" even of this earthly life. Eternity, we are asked to believe, is concerned with "fun and frolic", as though any man of character and intelligence would be content, even here, to give up a year of his life to "fun and frolic". This—and how much there is of it all round us—is worse than childishness; it is vulgar-minded worldliness. Its condemnation from the Christian point of view is already pronounced in the apostolic dictum that flesh and blood cannot inherit the Kingdom of God. When Christ told the Sadducees that in the resurrection they neither marry nor are given in marriage, He was not saying, as He has sometimes been understood to say, that the deepest and tenderest affections of human life are extinguished at death, but He was saying that even in the truest and noblest of them, as we know it in this life, there is bound up *something* which is of the earth earthy, and therefore is but for a time; they cannot be transferred, just as they stand, into the "eternal realm"; the best of them, in the continuance into eternity, must take on a touch of the "unearthly". If the pronouncement sounds austere, its austerity is of a kind that belongs to the whole Christian conception of the life to come. In the genuinely Christian life, even as it is lived by the Christian who is still in the flesh, there is always something unfamiliar and un-accountable, " wholly other ", from the point of view of a contented secularism; how much more must it be so when that life is continued into a state where the homely terrestrial environment so familiar to us here has finally fallen away. To forget this essential " otherness " of the " resurrection " life is intellectual vulgarity, though it is a vulgarity to which all of us are only too prone. But we are certainly thinking of eternal life unworthily, if it does not affect us with awe as well as with hope.

I do not mean, in these observations, to deny the truth which may well lie in the haunting suggestion of Milton's words:

> What if Earth
> Be but the shadow of Heav'n, and things therein
> Each to other like, more than on earth is thought?

It may be well so, and any man who has ever sat at the feet of Plato will say that it probably is so. But the point is that with every such likeness there must also go an unlikeness if Heaven is to be Heaven and Earth Earth, and that we, who are still wearing the image of the " earthy " man, do not know now what unlikeness subsists with what likeness. If we leave out the unlike-ness we are simply re-making Heaven in the form of a " fool's paradise " It is wisest and safest to commit ourselves only to one definite assertion, that to be in Heaven, as Christianity conceives of it, is to be a member of a society of persons who see God, themselves, and each other as all truly are, without confusion or illusion, and love God, themselves and each other with the love of this true insight; what is more than this is imaginative mythology, the fancies of men who are trying to see "in a glass darkly."

The great masters of the spiritual life illustrate this perfectly. When they write of Heaven and the state of the blessed, the points on which they dwell are commonly two: that God is seen there as He truly is, and is loved with utter devotion because He is seen to be wholly worthy of adoring love; the blessed see one another as persons whose personality has been re-made in the image of their Creator and Father, and love one another for this seen " likeness to God ". There are there none of the obstacles now put in the way of mutual understanding and love by the facts that our insight into ourselves and each other is so crudely imperfect, and that so much of what we do see in our not yet rightly re-made personality is unworthy of love. In our earthly house, where true personality has to be fashioned in the stress of conflict, even the best of us are hampered in insight and sympathy by the conditions of the conflict, which may force us, against our own will into competition and opposition. Here even the true saints may be condemned " by circumstances " to misunderstand each other. Where the conflict is no more these barriers are done away with. The one man knows at last what it was that the other " would be at " through those years of antagonism, and behold, it is nothing other than what he himself " would be at " all the while, and the old opponents are brothers and friends. So much the truly wise will allow themselves to be assured of; the sentimentalities of the popular descriptions of celestial joys they commonly leave to lesser men. *O quanta qualia sunt illa sabbata Quæ semper celebrat superna curia.* Yes, but the wise man does not attempt to specify the details of the " celebration "

The remarks of the last few paragraphs, however, are very much by the way, and may be said to be directed against a set of ideas not likely to have much weight with any one who contemplates human life in a proper temper of high moral seriousness. But there are certain ways of conceiving the destiny that lies before us which are certainly by no means wanting in moral seriousness, and yet cannot be said to be properly altogether Christian. Consider, for example, the eschatology of Plato. No philosopher has ever shown a temper of deeper moral seriousness; the doctrine of our immortality is of such importance in his eyes for two closely connected reasons; it intensifies our sense of the tremendous significance of every decision we make, for the right or the wrong, to be awake to the truth that every such choice has an influence on our whole moral being, not merely for some three-score years and ten, but for ever; " the issue whether we are to be really good or evil is a great one, far greater than it looks to be "; and again the answer to doubts of the justice of God raised in all of us by the spectacle of triumphant iniquity and oppressed goodness, which suggests that the universe is a moral chaos, is that when we take into the account the future hidden from us by the curtain of death we shall find that there is, in reality, a " judgment of God " from which none of us ever escape, and that this judgment is strictly according to our works. So far, as we listen to the voice of Plato, we seem to be hearing what is familiar to us as the doctrine of Christianity.

But when we come to study Plato's forecasts of human destiny more in detail, we begin to be aware of a difference. His view seems to be that while there are a few exceptional men who finally achieve " likeness to God " once and for all, and are thus, as Christianity

would say, at rest, and a few equally exceptional moral
" incurables " who are definitely " lost ", for the great
mass of mankind the future means a possibly infinite
succession of lives, in some of which they mount higher
in the scale of moral being, and in others sink lower,
without ever definitely achieving " salvation " or finally
forfeiting it. Our present life in the flesh is thus certainly
a period of educative training, and there is certainly a
divine moral judgment attending our use or misuse of
the training, but you cannot well say that, in the Platonic
conception, this life is in a special and peculiar sense one
of *probation*, or that the judgment of God is a *final*
judgment. Though there have been, and no doubt will
continue to be, attempts to incorporate this Platonic
eschatology into Christianity, it is a significant fact that
the general sense of the Christian Church has always been
against them. The religion which draws its deepest
inspiration from the New Testament has habitually
thought of the divine pronouncement on a man's life
as a *last* judgment, an irreversible sentence, and of our
life in time as a state of *probation* not to be repeated.
This so-called " porch " view of our present life may have
its difficulties, but it is too deeply inwoven into the
texture of the Christian religion to be disregarded.

We must not be misled here by the fact that there
are secondary divergences between Christian communities in their eschatology. Such disagreements do not
affect either the unique character of our life in time
as one of probation, nor the finality of the divine judgment on the individual when the time of probation is
ended. We must not, for example, credit Christians
who believe in " Purgatory " with the notion that
" Purgatory " is a sort of " second chance of making
good " offered to those who have not availed them-

selves of the first opportunity. It is part and parcel of the belief in Purgatory that its gates are open only to those who have made a right use of their " probation "; no one enters there who is not clearly, so to say, " ear-marked " for Paradise. The only point in dispute is, whether all of these, as a popular Protestant hymn puts it, " enter into immediate rest " at death, or whether, for most of them, this fruition of the joy of their Lord is, for God's good reasons, deferred; not whether the man who, during the time of probation, has, to the last, persistently turned away from God is to be given a " second chance ". We are not, of course, called upon to say of any man that he has done this, but it is definitely the Christian view that a man can do so if he will, and that if he does so, he is finally " lost ".

Thus our direction of our wills during the season of probation has from the Christian point of view an even more momentous significance than it has with Plato; it stamps each of us indelibly and for ever as " sheep " or as " goat ". This does not, of course, justify the really impious presumption of those bad Christians who take it upon themselves to pronounce this neighbour a " sheep " and that other a " goat ". The last judgment is not mine or yours but that of God " to whom all hearts are open, all desires known ". He may see obstinate alienation from Him where we cannot, as He may see an inward turning to Him which no human eye can detect. The appearances were certainly very much against Bunyan's Mr. Badman, yet Mr. Wiseman belies his name when he undertakes to pronounce with confidence that " Mr. Badman has gone to hell ". For, to one who stood too far off to catch the dying sentence, the appear-ances could have been no less against the penitent thief. That is an admirable story of the medieval friar who told his audience that there will be three great surprises in Heaven: the surprise of finding there so many whom we had never expected, the surprise of not finding so many whom we expected, and, most wonderful of all, the surprise of being there ourselves. The true use of the parable of the sheep and the goats is not to encourage us in presumptuous judgments on our fellows, but to awaken us to the danger of being among the goats ourselves.

But, it may be said, is there not something radically wrong with the whole conception of such a final division of mankind into the sheep and the goats? Is it not manifest that the more closely we look the more certainly we shall find that no one is either pure sheep or pure goat, all of us are a mixed breed? Certainly that is how things look to us, and it could not be otherwise. Since we are not infallible readers of hearts, even were the pure sheep or goat to be set before us, we could not certainly recognize them for what they were. And even if I *knew*, as I do not, the exact present state of my neighbour's heart towards God, I still could not know what it may yet become before the " accounts are made up ". But that is not the question. The real question is whether there is anything unreasonable in the view that when the life of temporal " making of ourselves " is surveyed as a completed whole by an omniscient Judge, it will not appear that some of us have " made our souls " into free personalities and others have not. A contemporary Italian philosopher [1] has some suggestive remarks on this point which it may be in place to reproduce in substance. He reminds us that men who have personally no belief in any judgment of God will confidently appeal in justification of conduct which is, as they claim, imper-

[1] A Guzzo: *Idealismo e Cristianismo.* ii, 251 ff.

fectly understood and misjudged by their contemporaries, to the " verdict of history "—that is, to the judgment of men in a later age who stand far enough removed from the present to view it without disturbing prejudices. When they are reminded that the men of the future will be often as ignorant and indifferent about the doings of to-day, and often as misinformed and full of prejudices of their own as the men of the eighteenth century were in their judgments on the Middle Ages—in a word, that the future which is to do equal justice to our careers seen as completed wholes and without bias is a future which never comes, the venue will be changed, and appeal made, it may be, to the verdict which " would have been given " by the venerated sages or heroes of the past. " Let the judgment on me ", so a man will say, " be that which Hampden or Montrose would have pro-nounced." [1] But that appeal too, we may retort, is a vain one. If the great men of the past could sit in session on me now, they would, of course, view me from the standpoint of their own age. A doctor of the thirteenth century would be as ill qualified to pronounce the final verdict on the life, say, of Voltaire as Voltaire for sitting in judgment on the doctor. It would seem, then, that, in the impossibility of finding a definitive judge of the present either in the past or in the future, a man must be finally referred—if a judgment of God is to be left out of the question—to the sentence of his own conscience. (Like Horace's Miser, he will say: *Populus me sibilat, at mihi plaudo*.) Thus we get the climax of unreason; the culprit at the bar claims also to be the omniscient and impartial judge on the bench, and absolves himself.

Well, the unreason is manifest enough, but no less manifest is the persistent and imperious demand of our

[1] The particular illustration is, of course, not Professor Guzzo's.

rational personality which has prompted it. Because a man is a rational being, he cannot avoid this sense of the necessity of a final sentence on himself and his works, passed on an unerring knowledge of those works as a completed series, and fixing their worth and his beyond the possibility of a revision of judgment. If he has lost belief in a real divine tribunal from which such a sentence is to proceed, he will still persist in the illusion that he can find a substitute for that tribunal in a future which can never come, in a past which has never been, in himself endowed with an omniscience and an equity which he knows he does not possess. The vitality of this demand for a *last* judgment of God is, indeed, not demonstration that such a judgment is a reality, but it is, at least, evidence that the belief in it is no mere illusion of a superstitious fancy but an exigence of our nature as reasonable itself. It should be taken into serious account by anyone who may be tempted to prefer the conception of a possibly endless succession of births and deaths to the Christian conception of the time of probation followed by a final judgment as the more *rational* of the two.

There is a precisely similar difference, which has often enough been remarked, between the Christian conception of the world's history as a whole and that of Plato, Aristotle, and many other non-Christian philosophers. As is generally well known, the Platonic and similar philosophies may offer us a vivid picture of the historical advance of man, in the period in which we are now living, from primitive helplessness and ignorance to a civilization based on the mastery over things which comes from knowledge. The history of the process is seen to have a *meaning*; it is not random variation, but variation tending steadily in the direction of the achievement of a rational life which has an inherent goodness and worth of its own. But, like all philosophies which teach the everlastingness of the natural world, Plato's can ascribe no such meaning and value to history as a *whole*. The gains of one cycle of the world's duration are only won to be lost again, and then the cycle begins anew, and this succession of alternate periods of ascent and descent repeats itself to infinity. The world, to put it crudely, is always " on the move " but it never " gets anywhere ". If we were to personify it, we should have to imagine it as a Sisyphus laboriously rolling his stone up the hill only to see it run back and to have to roll it up again. *Volvitur et volvetur in omne mutabilis aevum.* Each of the phases of the unending process is significant, but the whole has no significance: nothing " comes of it at last ". Greek philosophy, in consequence, never grasped, as our more modern way of thinking does, the uniqueness and " once-for-all-ness " of historical facts and characters. They could be thought of as presenting themselves " once for all " within a particular cycle of the world's duration, but they might recur indefinitely often in the endless succession of the cycles. Indeed some Greek philosophies went so far as to assert that every cycle repeats, down to the least detail, the whole history of every other. Thus Socrates, we say, drank the hemlock in a particular year which an Athenian calls the " year of Laches ", and dates as so many decades or centuries earlier than the year in which he is writing his narrative of the facts. But in truth, according to such philosophies, there has been not merely one " year of Laches " two thousand three hundred and thirty-six years before that in which I am writing these words; there have been an unknown number of such years, and will be an unknown number of them hereafter; in every one of them Socrates has drunk, or will yet drink, the hemlock. " The thing which hath been, it is that which shall be, and there is no new thing under the sun."

Very different is the spirit of our history, and even of our science. To us the names Julius Cæsar, or the Roman Empire, do not stand for a type of man or of society which has been seen a countless number of times in the past and will be seen as often in the future; they are names for a man and a society utterly and absolutely individual, which have appeared once in the world's past and will never be again. Even the revolutions of the heavenly bodies, as we now know, are not what Aristotle thought them, a wearying repetition of a fixed routine. This present revolution may be, for all practical purposes, indistinguishable from the last, but it is a repetition with a difference, and must be so unless the " principle of Carnot ", a very foundation-stone of our physical science, is false. A Greek might think of the " arrow of Time " as pointing indifferently forward or backward; the modern historian or scientific man can think of it as pointing only forward; to him the thing that has been is *never* the thing that shall be, and there is *always* something pointing only forward; to him the thing that has been is *never* the thing that shall be, and there is *always* something new under the sun so long as Time lasts.

Now there can be no reasonable doubt about the source of this heightened sense of the uniqueness of the historical; it has come to us as part of the inheritance of Christianity from its Hebrew origins. The Hebrews were not, like the Greeks, a people predisposed to philosophic and scientific thinking. The only book in the Old Testament canon which could conceivably be described as a philosophical work is *Ecclesiastes*, and the philosophical reflections of the writer who calls himself " King in Jerusalem ", to say nothing of their lack of genuine speculative depth, have all the appearances of being of Greek inspiration. But as historians the Hebrews, even of the days of the monarchy, show themselves to be admirably endowed. As Eduard Meyer has said, narratives like the description of Ahab's expedition against Ramoth-Gilead in 1 Kings, which bear every mark of being extracted from contemporary, or almost contemporary, compositions, have all the excellences of the best Greek historical writing; we look in vain for anything to compare with them in the remains of any other literature of the Near East. They are no mere annalistic records of accessions and demises, battles won and treaties concluded, but genuine pieces of history marked by the historian's insight into individual personality. It cannot be fanciful to connect this gift for the writing of history with the very strong sense of the personality of the nation's god so characteristic of the Hebrew. While the Greek usually tended to see in the march of affairs the realization of a pattern or plan which might be rational enough, in the sense of being orderly and intelligible but was not felt to be the expression of personal will, the Hebrew saw there first and foremost, a series of dramatic acts of will emanating from the Deity. The weak side of the Hebrew conception of God, we might say, is that it insists on His will at the expense of His reasonableness, sometimes to the point of representing that will as something formidable but capricious; the weakness of the Greek was that, in his conviction that " the divine " is orderly and rational, he tended to lose sight of the " personal drive " of the supreme world-ordering will. In the folk-lore of the Old Testament the " anger of the Lord " tends at times (as in the story of the migrations of the Ark, or that of David's attempted census) to sink to the level of a dangerous high explosive; with Plato, in spite of himself, the intrinsic reasonableness of the law that man fares according to his works is made so prominent that the personal will of which the law is the appointment tends to fall into the background. Possibly this standing Greek predisposition to over-emphasize the cognitive, as compared with the conative, aspect of intelligent life may explain why it is that the greatest names among the Greek historians belong to the time before the Hellenic genius had become fully clear to itself about its true native bent. In all the centuries of the domination of the Greek mind by philosophy, from Socrates to Proclus, there was no second Thucydides.

Be that as it may, it seems clear at least that our modern sense of the uniqueness and " once-for-all-ness " of the historical event, which, because historical, never recurs, is a legacy from the Hebrews with their dramatic interpretation of the course of time as a sequence of " mighty acts " of the Creator leading up to an all along foreseen and intended climax. It is only the incongruity of " endless cyclical recurrence " with this notion of what Tennyson loosely calls the " increasing " purpose underlying the march of events—he meant, presumably, a purpose which becomes increasingly discernible by *us* as it draws to its full embodiment—which makes the conception of " recurrences " an absurdity. (It is quite impossible to prove it false by any appeal to " scientific fact ". The most that the " principle of Carnot " can tell us is that, so far as we can see, the system of nature is " running down "; it is beyond our power to see how, when once " run down ", it can be wound up again, but not more beyond our power than it is to see how it could ever have come into the condition which we have to presuppose as that from which it is running down. We can only account for the fact that the amount of cosmic

energy " available for work " is not already exhausted
by presuming in the remote past a distribution of that
energy which is " infinitely improbable ".) The case
being so, the strength of our conviction that the course
of time is irreversible affords, at any rate, some presumption that the belief in divine purpose necessary to
the justification of that conviction is no illusion but a
glimpse into truth. If then it is reasonable to think of
the whole history of the universe as the manifestation
of a coherent purpose, and as therefore having a goal,
it is not unreasonable to think the same thing about our
own personal history. No one should lightly reject the
Christian conception of our own life as issuing in the
definitive winning or losing of " eternal salvation " on the
ground of the alleged superior reasonableness of the indefinite alternation of birth and death, unless he is prepared
to pronounce the ancient belief in the " cyclical recurrence " of the history of the universe more rational than
our modern conception of the uniqueness of historical fact.[1]

If our present life as persons whose personality is still

[1] The force of this reasoning should not be overestimated. It
aims merely at showing that the traditional Christian belief as a *final*
judgment on our lives and characters is congruous, as the notion
of indefinitely repeated alternations of birth and death is not, with
our modern scientific belief in the irreversibility of the temporal
order; we are not here attempting to answer anyone who denies this
irreversibility. And our references to *purpose* must not be misunderstood as though we were asserting that the divine end, or purpose,
is something only exhibited by the last term in the series of events
which make up the history of a universe or a person. We should
conceive of it rather as showing itself in and controlling the course
of the whole series. It is in this sense that a great work of art—the
tragedy of *Hamlet*, for example—exhibits purpose in the author.
The " catastrophe " in which the tragedy ends is not related to the
events out of which it arises, as the dwelling-house is to the scaffolding
employed in its construction and removed when the work is complete.
The purpose of the dramatist is not merely to lead up to the final
scene, but to exhibit, all through the play, a human character reacting

" in the making " and not fully made is, as Christianity,
holds it is, a " state of probation ", it seems necessary,
then, to hold that the probation must have had a beginning and will have an end. Such a statement still
leaves unanswered many questions which intellectual
curiosity suggests and which were, in fact, canvassed by
the early Fathers of the Church. There is, for example,
the question on which St. Augustine seems never to
have come to a definite conclusion, how the personal
life of each of us began. Is personality transmitted by
generation from parents to children, or is it originated,
for each of us, by a special creative act of God, and in
that case, does this act take place, for each of us, some
few months before his birth, or were all souls created
" in the beginning ", though their moral histories were
only to take shape in the course of successive generations,
as they were embodied? It may well be doubted whether
such a question permits of a definite answer from our
" natural reason ", and it would be difficult to maintain
that the Christian scriptures commit themselves to any

to the situations in which it is placed in a way which calls for that
finale. But the point is that if the play is to be informed throughout
with purpose in this fashion, there must be a " last scene of all ".
If *Hamlet* went on with scene after scene interminably, though a single
scene, or a single group of scenes might have the kind of purposive
unity necessary to a work of art, the play could not have it. As a
whole, it would " get nowhere ".

It may be worth noting that our heightened modern sense of the
" once-for-all-ness " of all historical events removes a difficulty which
was often expressed, in less historically-minded times, in connection
with the Christian doctrine of the Incarnation of the Son of God. It
used to be said: " But why one Incarnation in this particular region
of space and time? Why not rather possibly innumerable Incarnations
(or, rather, avatars)? " The answer is that the supposed persons in
whom these incarnations were embodied would, if the incarnations
are all that Christianity means by the word, be actually identical,
and that if the historical is really unique, there can no more be two
such persons than there can be two Julius Cæsars.

pronouncement on so purely speculative a question. Similarly, we might ask a question about the way in which the "state of probation" is brought to an end. It is not immediately evident that its end must coincide with the death of the body, and the general consensus of Christians that this is so is, no doubt, based simply on the fact that in the main the New Testament writers seem to make that assumption, though it is rarely, if ever at all, explicitly enunciated, and there are one or two passages here and there in the New Testament which, if taken by themselves, might be held to point the other way. (Thus we read in the Gospel of a sin which has no remission in this life or in that which is to come; and it might be suggested that the implication is that other sins which have not found remission in this life may obtain it hereafter. And there are the well-known sentences of 1 Peter about the preaching to "the spirits in prison" and to the "dead" who had been disobedient in the days of Noah. But it must be remembered that these are isolated passages, that they admit of more than one exegesis, and that whatever interpretation we put upon them, we should be guided in our understanding of Christianity by the sense of the New Testament as a whole.)

Fortunately, for our purposes, it is not necessary to enter into a discussion of questions which are perhaps insoluble, and on which the writer of these pages would feel it an impertinence to obtrude mere personal impressions of his own. He could only repeat that if we are to be true to the spirit of Christianity, any opinions we may allow ourselves to hold provisionally and tentatively on such matters must be such as are compatible with the recognition of a "state of probation" which does not endure indefinitely and of a judgment of God which is veritably a *last* judgment.

VII

IT will profit us more to consider certain attacks which have been made on the Christian conceptions in the very interests of genuine morality and religion themselves. To deal first with the objection which has often been taken on strictly ethical grounds: virtue, it said, to be genuine virtue must be disinterested; the virtuous man does what is right because it is right, and loves what is good because it is good, not for the sake of any ulterior advantage or profit to be got for himself out of virtue. Virtue pursued for its "consequences"; or with a view to avoiding the undesirable consequences of vice, is not really virtue at all; you cannot be virtuous for hire. But Christianity, it is complained, has taught men to think of right living, immorally, as a " serving of God for pay ", for it represents the gaining of " celestial bliss " or the avoidance of the torments of Gehenna as the *motive* for good and dutiful action. A man is, then, to do right with an eye to getting his " crown in Heaven " (or escaping the danger of getting his reward for acting otherwise in hell). And thus, as Kant complained, the introduction of the " religious sanction " entirely destroys the sublimity of the moral law. It is sublime only so long as it is venerated for itself without any reference to " consequences ".

Now it ought to be clear that this reasoning is un-assailable so far as the principle upon which it is based is concerned. A virtue which has as its motive not love of good but a calculation of personal gain is not really virtue at all, any more than the so-called financial probity which a man practises simply because he is afraid of exposure, or penal servitude, is honesty. If I discharge my functions as a trustee without fraud or embezzlement *only* from the consideration that in all probability fraud or embezzlement would land me in prison, my accounts may be correct to the last farthing, but I am already dishonest at heart. I think it must also be conceded that too many Christians have allowed themselves to use language about their expected " rewards " in the world to come which, if it really represented their true state of mind, would fairly lay them open to the charge of debasing the moral currency. It is distressing, for example, to find Berkeley treating Shaftesbury's insistence on the disinterestedness of real virtue as a target for the shafts of his sarcasm.[1] Still, it is fair to remember that what Berkeley really has in mind is less Shaftesbury's moral theory than the moral practice of contemporary free-thinkers who have Shaftesbury's language about the beauty of disinterested virtue continually on their lips. What he really means to urge against the deist Alciphron is not that virtue should be practised as a means to rewards hereafter, but that the standard of disinterested virtue attained by men who have dismissed from their minds the thought of answerability to the judgment of God, is not likely to be a high one. His contention would lose none of its weight if we removed from it all reference to " rewards " and worded it thus: the mere conviction that disinterested doing of good because it is good is a fine and beautiful thing will not stand a man in good stead in the conflict with the severer temptations of life unless it is joined with the sense of imperative and inescapable *obligation*. The real point Berkeley and those who use language like his

[1] *Alciphron*, Dialogue iii.

intend to make is precisely that which Kant expresses so perfectly when he insists that we do not serve in the ranks of duty like gentlemen volunteers, free to distinguish ourselves if we please, but also free to take our ease, or to absent ourselves when we choose; we are all " privates " of the regular forces, subject to the full discipline of the camp. The distinction is absolutely sound, and to call attention to it is not in any way to degrade virtue into mere interested serving for hire.

The true issue at stake is this, and it is a momentous one: can we divorce practical morality from the " religious sanction " without striking a deadly blow at the vital principle of virtue itself? And in asking the question we need to be clear about its exact meaning. It does not mean " can a man do right without expecting to be paid for it here or hereafter? " Those who, like myself, believe that the religious sanction is inseparable from a vigorously flourishing morality do not understand by the " religious sanction " anything so crude as " rewards or penalties believed to be bestowed or inflicted here or hereafter by God for virtuous or vicious conduct ". What we do mean is simply that it is fatal to the moral life to look upon right-doing as no more than a fine and honourable achievement, or a desirable accomplishment; right-doing is an absolute and imperative obligation. In our opinion recognition of *absolute* obligation logically involves recognition of a supreme superhuman Lord of spirits to whom we are answerable for the use we make of life. We do not deny the manifest fact that there are individual men who have lost belief in the Supreme Judge but retain the sense of moral obligation unimpaired. None of us, probably, is ever fully aware of all that is logically implied by his own convictions, and so the " fear of God " may be a genuine influence in the life of a man who is not even aware that he believes in God. But sooner or later, however slowly and gradually the logical implications of man's convictions come to be apprehended, and thus a radical change in beliefs leads to a corresponding change in practices. Sooner or later, then, it will be generally seen that if there is no Most High to whom we are answerable, there can be no eternal moral law, and no absolute obligation, and when absolute obligation is no longer recognized genuine morality itself will have perished. Nothing will be left in its stead but " commandments of men " made by our predecessors to suit their temporary convenience and liable to be refashioned quite differently by their successors to suit *their* convenience. The practical inference will be drawn that, as a character in a novel published a few years ago coarsely put it: " There's no old Mumbo-Jumbo of a God to prevent our doing as we please." Persons who think thus may still " please " to show a good deal of kindness and consideration for one another (at least when it does not cost them very much to do so), but in such a state of general opinion genuine *morality* would be on its death-bed. The rejection of the " religious sanction " would have had the very effect charged by Kant upon those who degrade it into a matter of bribes and threats; in a society where obedience was only shown because men " pleased " to show it, and as long as they " pleased ", the moral law would have " lost all its sublimity ".

Also it should, of course, be added that whatever may have been said at any time by particular Christians, every actual Christian is a very imperfect Christian, and we are not to take his utterances as they stand as expressions of the true spirit of Christianity. They may do it grievous injustice, just as the language of actual individual

" patriots ", with its everlasting note of national self-glorification, aggressiveness and prejudice against the " foreigner ", would be a wrong standard by which to judge the moral value of a true love of one's country and people. The people of England are perhaps freer than any other in the world from the baser kind of " nationalism ", yet which of them would not be in danger of pitching a good deal of a " patriotic oration " in a false and unworthy key? And it is a good deal harder to live habitually at the genuine Christian level of thought and emotion than it is to be an ideally " good Englishman ". We must judge of Christianity in this matter by the ideal it sets before us and the demands that ideal makes of us, not by our inadequate attempts to rise to it. When we apply this test, it should be plain at once that Christianity, as distinguished from the faulty practice of very imperfect Christians, is clear of the charge of debasing the moral currency. The Christian law, as laid down for us by the Author of our religion, is no law of outward performance. What it demands from us is an inward and habitual state of the affections and the will; we are, in the first place, to love God with our whole heart and mind, and, in the second, to love our neighbour as ourselves. It is involved in the very statement of the command that obedience to it must be " disinterested ". We are—and all the great expositors of Christianity have been careful to insist on the point— to love God for Himself, for what He is, because He is the one adequate object of a love that knows no reserves, not for anything to be got out of Him. A professed love of God which is no more than " cupboard love " is not love of God, but only love of His gifts. The man who " loved God ", if there could be such a man, for the sake of a " reward " in the life to come would not really be loving *God*, and therefore would not get the reward. And as to the love of our neighbour, though it is true that Christ promises us that it will have its reward, He does not tell us that the desire of the reward is to be the motive of our love. On the contrary, we are to do good to our neighbour " hoping for nothing again ". The rewards of which the Gospel speaks are only to be had on the condition that it is God and our neighbour, not the rewards, upon which our hearts are set.

The same thing is equally true if we consider the nature of the reward promised. The reward offered for love of God and our neighbour is " eternal life ", and all that is definitely told us of that life is that it consists in knowledge and love of God. The " pay ", if we may call it so, for loving God is to be that hereafter we shall be able to love Him better because we shall have a more unclouded vision of Him; the " pay " for loving our neighbour is a life in which we shall be able to love him more because we shall understand him and ourselves more intimately. Now this is a kind of reward which could have no appeal to the supposed " interested self-seeker ". If you do not already genuinely love God and your neighbour with a " disinterested " love, it is no inducement to try to do so to be told that your reward will be a greater capacity of loving, just as, to a man who had not already the artist's or scholar's love of beauty or knowledge for themselves, it would be no inducement to undergo the drudgery of the artistic or scholarly life to promise that it would be recompensed in the end by the insight of the master in art or scholarship.

Christianity does not deny the proposition that " virtue is its own reward ", in any sense in which the statement is true. It explains its meaning by saying that the " re-

ward " of goodness practised under all hindrances and
drawbacks of our present state of being is goodness
exhibited in a life where there is no longer anything to
thwart it, within us or without us. As the theologians
have put it, the one " essential " joy of heaven is the
knowledge and love of God itself, the " beatific vision ";
everything else is consequential and " accidental ". But
the supposed server of God for hire does not at heart
care about knowing and loving God, but only about
something totally different which he imagines he may get
as " pay " Clearly, then, if he could be transported to
Heaven itself, its " joys " would not be joys to him; he
would be as unhappy as the proverbial fish out of water.
He would be still more uncomfortable than he can be on
earth, for here he can often forget that God sees him as
he is, with all his petty self-centredness, and he can be
reasonably sure that his neighbours can be imposed upon;
in Heaven he would be completely " found out ". And
what is more, he would inevitably find himself out, and
the discovery would not be a pleasing one. Where everyone " knows as he is known ", the self-seeker could no
longer even take himself in, as the best of us contrive to
do here. He would have to see himself for the worthless
fellow he is.

The charge against Christianity which we have been
discussing would probably never have been put forward
by any serious student and critic if Christians had always
been as mindful as they should be of their own professed
doctrine that to the " saved " who enjoy the direct vision
of God in Heaven, it is the vision itself, not any con-
comitants it may bring with it, which is the source of
their blessedness. They are happy because they have their
heart's desire; if what their hearts have been set on had
been some private and particular gratification of which

any of them could feel ' it is *mine*, and being mine is therefore not *yours* ', the Christian Heaven would not provide them with their heart's desire and they would not be happy there. Tennyson falsifies the thought of Christianity when he makes Arthur add to the expression of his hope that Guinevere may yet meet him in Paradise, the suggestion that there she will be his, " not Lancelot's nor another's ". *All* the " saints in Paradise "—and Lancelot was in the end to be one of them—are one another's, because all are God's; it is part of the temporary necessities of our state of " pilgrimage " that there must be *des amitiés particulières*, so that I can only be all I ought to be to one person by being something less to others. But to imagine these limitations and exclusiveness to be continued into the life of the soul which has reached its true home is, in Dante's phrase, not to understand the meaning of Christ's *neque nubent*. Earthly life must have its exclusivenesses, but those who would extend them to the eternal world are going as far astray in one direction as those who propose to dispense with them here in the other.

VIII

IT would not be honest to evade what has been, and perhaps in many quarters still is, the gravest ground of the dissatisfaction felt by so many of the best men with the Christian doctrine of the future life, the traditional account given of the state of the finally "lost". It has been depicted as one of unending and excruciating torture, bodily and mental, without even the prospect of a merciful dulling of sensibility as suffering becomes habitual. And it has sometimes been asserted that this fate awaits not merely bad Christians and persons who, having had the truths of Christianity clearly set before them, have deliberately shut their eyes to them, but all the countless millions of those who have never heard of Christianity, and could not have heard of it—the pagans of the past, the multitudes who pass their lives at the present day in regions to which Christianity has never penetrated, even, according to the most extreme form of the theory, all unbaptized infants, whose only fault is the misfortune of being, by no choice of their own, born into a world which had been poisoned by the misdoing of their remotest ancestors. Such a doctrine, it is said, is a monstrous libel on a Creator who is declared officially to be a God of love, or indeed, on any ruler of men who is more than a mercilessly cruel autocrat; if it were true, an honest man, knowing it to be true, would be driven to refuse his love and worship to such a deity and face the consequences of the refusal to himself.

Now it is true that much Christian literature throughout the ages has taught things of this kind; there is a type of " religious " book dealing with the fate of the " lost " which is morally simply repulsive, and for which it is better to offer no apology. But it is by no means clearly realized by many of those who make the traditional pictures of hell a reproach to Christianity, that very little of all this has ever received the full imprimatur of the authority of the whole Church, and that most of it would be certain to be repudiated by all Christian bodies of any consequence at the present day. We must be careful not to confuse the Christian faith with the theories of theologians, however eminent, in the past and the present.

It is worthy of notice that neither in the Nicene Creed nor in the Apostles' Creed is anything definite said about the state of the " lost ". It is asserted that there is a judgment of God upon all of us, and is plainly implied that that judgment is final and decisive, but beyond this we are told nothing, and we are not to take assent to the statements of these creeds about the judgment as in any way committing a Christian to belief in the lurid fancies of too many theologians about the torture-chambers of Gehenna. And apart from these two great creeds there are no other documents which possess the same claim to represent the deliberate and authoritative teaching of the undivided Church. Hence it is not surprising that there should at all times, even in days when men's minds were most possessed by the imagination of a Gehenna of torments, have been eminent theologians whose views were of a very different kind. To say nothing of Origen, whose speculations were generally disavowed by the Church, it seems to have been the conviction of some of the most distinguished Greek Fathers that, sooner or later, all men, even the most hardened, will find salvation; and the passages of the New Testament which seem to speak in a different sense must be understood as we understand the warnings of a physician or the threats of the law. The physician warns us of the consequences of neglecting his directions, as the legislator threatens us with the penalties for breach of his laws, precisely that we may take his admonitions to heart, with the result that the threatened penalties, or the foretold sufferings, are not in fact inflicted. If either had it in his power to impress our minds as deeply as he could wish, he would desire that his threat or warning should do its work so effectually as to remain unfulfilled. So, it was sometimes said, God's warnings, or threats, of the consequences of obstinate alienation of heart and will from Him have no other purpose than to prevent that alienation with all its consequences. Being good, this is what He desires and intends, and since He has the power to work directly upon the inmost motions of men's souls, we may at least hope that, unlike the human physician or legislator, He will meet with no hopeless incurables or utter incorrigibles. In the end, we may trust, all of us will find our way back to Him, by rough ways or by smooth. A universalism of this kind, which is something very different from the unethical light-hearted universalism of some modern writers, though it cannot be said ever to have won general recognition from the Church, does not seem to be formally incompatible with the strictest " orthodoxy ". Since it is the universal doctrine of Christians that the sinner *may* turn from the evil of his way at the last moment of the eleventh hour, and that only the Reader of all hearts can know of any sinner that he has died " finally impenitent ", no Christian Church can take it on itself to pronounce of any man that he has actually been " lost ". At most it can only say that *if* any man has died in a state of final rebellion against God, that

man has been " lost "; whether this has actually happened, and to whom, can be known only to the divine
omniscience. The point of practical importance for each
of us is that, even though it should never have happened
before, it is possible that it may happen with me, if I
persist in wilfulness or sloth.

It is forgotten also, in much that is written against the
Christian traditional teaching about the " last things ",
that the extremely dark picture we have outlined above
does not faithfully represent the main body of instructed
theological opinion throughout the ages. The horrible
Augustinian theory of the endless suffering of unbaptized
infants is a corollary of the extreme Augustinian doctrine
of original sin, according to which the transgression of
the progenitor of our race makes it just that all his
posterity should suffer endlessly for their first father's
fault. But this peculiar interpretation of " original sin "
was a speculation of Augustine's own devising: it has
apparently never been accepted in the Eastern Church,
and was profoundly modified in the Western by the
great schoolmen. The standing doctrine of the Western
Church all through the Middle Ages was that though
unbaptized infants, not having been initiated into the
fellowship of Christ by baptism, are incapable of the
vision of God which constitutes the essential bliss of the
redeemed, this exclusion from a supernatural boon of
which the infant is wholly unaware, is the only penalty
it pays for " the sin of Adam "; there is, as the phrase
was, no further " sensible penalty ". Clearly such a
theory permits of holding that the future of unbaptized
children is one of great and real " natural " happiness,
though it is not the best, the happiness of knowing God
as He is. There is no community of Christians to-day, it
may safely be said, which thinks of the future of these

innocents, as Augustine did, as one of suffering and unhappiness.

There is also much confusion, even in the minds of some who ought to be better informed, about the future of the " virtuous heathen ". I do not know whether the problem was seriously considered by the early Fathers, but it was actually much in the minds of the theologians of the Middle Ages, who were keenly conscious of their debt to the ancient philosophers, and their teaching on the point is quite clear. The doctrine of St. Thomas, for example, is that it is certain that " gentiles " have been saved (a notable case being, as is carefully pointed out, that of the patriarch Job), and St. Thomas adds that we may be quite sure that any " gentile " who manifested the due disposition to embrace the truth, if once made known to him, *was* saved; God either sent a messenger to instruct him, or directly enlightened him by a revelation of what was necessary. Dante is thus expressing the sense of medieval orthodoxy perfectly correctly when he places the Trojan warrior Rhipæus, Virgil's *iustissimus unus*, high in Paradise. In fact the men of the thirteenth century were so far from asserting the damnation of the " virtuous heathen " that Roger Bacon finds it in place to caution his hearers against an opposite temerity; they must not, he says, positively affirm as a fact the salvation of Aristotle or other pagan philosophers, because though the fact may well be as they say, they cannot know it to be so. It is possible that any or all of these great pagans are among the saved, if in their lifetime they had humility and charity; but whether they had these graces is God's secret which has not been disclosed to us.

Whether the medieval theologians would have been ready to give the benefit of this doctrine to " virtuous unbelievers " living *after* the promulgation of the Gospel

I cannot profess to know, but Dante clearly did not anticipate that he would be giving any offence by representing Moslems like Saladin and Averroes as sharing the limbo of the sages and heroes of antiquity with Aristotle and Virgil. And whatever the personal judgments of medieval doctors may have been, it is certain that at no time has the Christian Church committed itself to any dogma of the damnation of the " virtuous unbeliever ", and that no Christian society of any account believes anything of the kind to-day.

(The eighteenth Article of the Anglican Church, which has sometimes been brought up in this connection, is quite irrelevant. What is condemned there is the assertion that " every man shall be saved by the law or sect which he professeth ". What is meant is not that no Jew or no Moslem will be saved, but simply that if he is saved it will not be *because* he was a Jew or a Moslem; that Moses and Mahomet are not rival saviours to Christ for those who happen to be born Jews or Turks; Jews or Turks, if they are saved, will, like the rest of us, be saved by the grace of the one Saviour of the world. Not to dwell on the obvious consideration that, in any case, the Thirty-nine Articles are not a creed, but a mere list of points upon which the Convocation of the year 1562 judged it desirable to prohibit controversy.)

Still, it may be said, when all the necessary conditions of popular anti-Christian rhetoric have been duly made, the main objection urged by the unfavourable critic holds good. We may set aside the cases of infants and " virtuous unbelievers ", and confine ourselves to that of persons who, with full opportunity of knowing what their Creator has designed them for and what He asks of them, still from obstinate perversity or indifference or idleness disregard the drawings of His love. The real

problem is the future of those who have been awakened
to hear the divine message and have neglected it, not
that of those who have never heard it at all. The servant
who knew his master's will and left it undone, we are
told in the Gospel, will be beaten with many stripes. But
if we seriously believe in the fundamental Christian conception of God as being, before everything else, Love, can
we suppose the " many stripes " to mean unending and
inexpressible tortures? Can a God of love have designed
oubliettes for even the worst among His creatures? There
is the question which the Christian Church never fully
faced until very recent times, though, as Butler says
about a different problem which moralists in his day
were trying to shirk, " surely it is to be put ". For my
own part, I can see only one possible answer, when the
issue is fairly raised. If God be what the Christian religion
declares that He is, if He has the character on the strength
of which it pronounces Him worthy of supreme and
unqualified love from men, we simply cannot credit Him
with the infliction of these tortures upon anything His
hands have made. Nor do either the New Testament or
the great confessions of faith which express the sense of
Christianity upon its " fundamentals " really require us
to do so.

The point upon which both the New Testament and
the creeds of the Church are explicit is that there is a
judgment of God upon all of us, and that, as we have
said, this judgment is final and irreversible; what goes
beyond this single statement can claim to be no more
than the " pious (or unfortunately, perhaps the impious)
opinion " of this or that other theologian. The great
creeds are notoriously silent about everything except the
reality and finality of the divine judgment. (I do not
consider here the concluding " damnatory " clauses of

the *Quicunque Vult*, since that document has never enjoyed
an authoritative position throughout the whole of Chris-
tendom.) The language of the New Testament, when
we look at it closely, is often emphatic about the finality
of the judgment, but is singularly reticent as to the
precise doom of those who stand finally condemned.
The metaphorical language in which their exclusion from
eternal life is expressed is, for the most part, when we
remember that it is frankly metaphorical, compatible
either with the continued existence of the " lost " in their
unfortunate condition or with complete and irreversible
destruction. We hear, for example, of the " unquench-
able fire ", but we have to remember, when we try to
interpret the metaphor, that fire is employed primarily
for two purposes: the refinement of materials that can be
refined, and the destruction of refuse; even among men,
it is only the tyrant and oppressor who employs fire as a
medium of torture. And the New Testament references
to the " fire " are, on the face of them, mostly allusions to
a particular passage of the Old Testament (Isaiah lxvi. 24)
where the original thought is clearly that of destruction,
not of torment. (The prophet is declaring that when
Israel attains its final deliverance, the carcases of the
enemies who have beset Jerusalem will be consumed in
the valley of Hinnom, outside the walls of the city—not
that these enemies will be tortured.) The real source of
the most lurid pictures of future torments in which
preachers in various ages have revelled is not the Gospels,
but the Apocalypse. It is there only that we read of a
" lake of fire " and of victims who are thrown alive into
it and " tormented " unceasingly. Apparently this fate is
only foretold there for two offenders, the " beast " and
the " false prophet ", and it may fairly be said that these
are not so much individual historical sinners as symbolic

personification of the Roman Empire, organized as a persecuting, anti-Christian " totalitarian state ", and its idolatrous false religion. We are not really entitled to draw any inference from such passages about the future which awaits the individual man or woman. When we set these apocalyptic passages on one side, there does not seem to be any utterance of the New Testament which depicts the state of the man who has failed to achieve salvation as one of endless excruciating torment.

And, whatever Christians have allowed themselves to imagine in the past, it is probably safe to say that these horrible representations of the sufferings of the impenitent do not express the views of any section of Christians of the present day considerable enough to deserve notice. It would be truer to say that Christians of to-day are agreed that their religion teaches the possibility of a final and irreparable loss of eternal life, and to leave the matter there. They recognize that in any life which is not merely frivolous there is the possibility of tragedy, and that any theory which eliminates that possibility from the ultimate scheme of things is simply superficial. But the presence of tragedy in the scheme of the universe and the possibility that any one of us may, by his own wilfulness or negligence, make an irreparable tragedy of his own life do not require us to credit the God of infinite love with the deliberate infliction of excruciating torture on life's failures. How in detail God deals with these failures we neither know nor need to know. But we may at least be sure that if it is indeed true that His mercy is over all His works, even the failures are not outside the compass of His love.[1]

[1] I am indebted here particularly to some remarks on this point by the Bishop of London (Dr. Winnington Ingram) in a small composite volume entitled *Asking Them Questions* (Oxford University Press,

It is sometimes said by unscrupulous or unreflecting anti-Christian controversialists, that such views are only an adulterated version of Christianity, and that to be sincerely Christian we must be prepared to accept the most frightful imaginations of the Middle Ages, as they are preserved for us; for example, by the horrible pictures on the walls of the Campo Santo of Pisa, or in the cantos of Dante's *Inferno*. But this contention will not really bear examination. If what is meant by a genuine unadulterated Christianity is adherence to the express utterance of the New Testament, as we have already said, the horrors of the Dantesque Inferno are not really to be found there. They represent, at best, an interpretation put on the New Testament by the men of past ages. The men who interpreted the New Testament thus were members of societies which saw nothing amiss in the infliction of lingering and inhuman tortures upon offenders by human courts of " justice ". It did not outrage their moral feelings that a human being or judge should burn a criminal alive in a slow fire, break him to pieces on the wheel, or disembowel and mutilate his living body, and they quite consistently imagined divine justice as doing the same thing on a larger scale. Their theory and their practice, good or bad, were coherent. With us it is quite different. Whatever the Christian of to-day may profess to believe about the fate of a bad man in the unseen world, he would think himself, if he burned the worst of criminals alive, morally

1936; pp. 180–181).   I may quote one or two sentences: " In these three points hell is like Gehenna.   It is outside the holy city; secondly, it is a place where the morally infectious are kept from harming others; but (thirdly), it is not outside the government of the great and loving God.   In other words, God is the God of hell as well as the God of heaven. . . . Those who are in hell, whatever hell is, are still under the government and under the care of God."

worse than his victims. He thinks himself bound, even when it is a duty to put a grave offender to death, to avoid the infliction of gratuitous torment. There is a passage in a story by Mr. Eden Philpotts where an eighteenth-century judge refuses to interest himself in a proposal for making English methods of capital execution more humane (presumably by the introduction of the " drop ") on the ground that " the law does not mean " a thief to have an easy and speedy death; it intends the protraction of suffering for its own sake. To-day, I take it, all of us would agree that such a sentiment is as un-Christian as it is inhuman. And the proof that we are sincere is that we have long ago reformed our practice in the matter, and the reform was made by men who were Christians. But a man who holds that he would be guilty of a barbarity if he burned an offender for a quarter of an hour, but also maintains that He who is the author alike of justice and mercy will burn the same offender for endless millions of years is *not* consistent with himself—except on the supposition that he is prepared to add that the God of perfect justice and perfect mercy is the supreme barbarian. If we are not to go back to the practice of the *siècles d'égorgeurs, de lâches, et de brutes*, how can we consistently accept as authoritative a " gloss " in the meaning of the New Testament inspired in them by their own bad practices? And if we are to commit ourselves to medievalism of this kind, let us do so in no half-hearted fashion. If we must have fire, and worms and brimstone, let them be, as the men of the Middle Ages insisted that they were, " material " fire, worms, and brimstone endowed with properties—such as those of directly preying on the mind, or of burning without destroying—quite at variance with their " material " character. But in fact we ought to be more trustworthy interpreters of the New Testament than our medieval progenitors could be. How adequately a man will conceive of the divine justice and the divine mercy depends on the quality of his own justice and his own mercy, and what was the mercy and justice of the Middle Ages we know from the record of history.

It would be no defence of the kind of medievalism we are now discussing to say, as has been said by its belated defenders, that the argument of the foregoing paragraph confuses retribution with restraint, or with reformatory discipline, and so misses its mark. For, we are told, retribution (and the doom of evil men in the next world is purely retributory) is suffering inflicted for wrong done in the past; the suffering is justified simply by the fact that the wrong has been done, and therefore to speak of it as "useless", and so to imply that it has, or ought to have, any end to serve, is irrelevant or, to put the point more plainly, suffering inflicted as retribution has no end beyond that of exacting from an offender the debt which he has incurred. I will not here enter on the wider and difficult question how far it is a satisfactory view of punishment, whether human or divine, to regard it as purely retributory in this sense. For the purpose of argument let us agree to concede that the punishments of a world to come are to be thought of in that light. It will follow, at once, that to be just the payment exacted must bear a proportion to the debt. We are therefore faced with the question whether unending torture can conceivably be a payment which bears just proportion to any debt a human being can incur, however grievously he may have offended. It has, indeed, been argued that any offence whatsoever against the law of God, being an affront to one who is of infinite majesty, must be an infinitely great offence and calls for an infinite payment in suffering. But this reasoning is plainly sophistical, since it would equally justify any monarch in treating all offences against his law as high treason and visiting them with the penalties of treason. It is therefore not surprising that St. Thomas, the greatest theologian of the Middle Ages, would have nothing to say to this argument. The punishment of the impenitent, he said, is in one way infinite, since it is eternal and irreversible, but it is irreversible because their impenitence itself is irreversible; in another sense it is not infinite, but proportioned to the magnitude of their guilt, as indeed we are told in the New Testament itself. The distinction here taken between the irreversibility of the divine sentence and the " infinity " of its effects must surely be pronounced to be on exactly the right lines; the pity of it is that St. Thomas, being after all a man of the thirteenth century, virtually nullifies his own distinction when he comes to employ his imagination in constructing a picture of hell; he allows himself to forget that even the offender who is beaten with the fewest stripes, on his showing, suffers an unending succession of bitter tortures, and that the sum of such an infinite series " increase beyond every finite maximum ".

Yet the medieval theologians themselves lay down principles which might well have provided a way of escape from the dreadful imagination of the divine torturer. They are agreed that the supreme evil endured by the inmates of hell is not to be found in any of its supposed torments; it is the lost soul's knowledge that, by its own fault, it has put itself for ever out of all possibility of attaining the vision of God; it has definitely missed the end for which it was made and without which it can never be satisfied and at peace. The " fixed aversion of the will from God " is thus a sin which proves to be its own punishment. It is not strictly true that in this present life " vice is its own punishment ", for so long as a man is in the body, it is possible for him to blind himself to the ends for which he has been created; he can temporarily delude himself into the notion that worldly pleasure, or wealth, or rank, or power, is the food which will satisfy the soul's hunger. But when he has left this life behind him, his eyes are opened; he learns now that none of these things can satisfy an immortal being made in the image of God; he learns also that there is something very different which would satisfy the spirit, and he knows that he has wantonly forfeited that satisfaction for ever; that is his tragedy. If one has imagination enough to conceive the state of one who has made that discovery, one realizes, I think, that this very knowledge that one has " like the base Indian thrown a pearl away Richer than all his tribe " is, in itself, a fate too tragic to require farcing with dreams of material or quasi-material horrors which it is dishonouring the God and Father of our Lord Jesus Christ to impute to Him. Shelley may have meant to be flippant—though flippancy was not congenial to him—when he wrote that " It is a lie to say *God damns* ", but there was truth at the bottom of the words. God does not cast into Hell as an Eastern sultan might cast a wretch, who had provoked his anger, to the lions; it is the persistently rebellious sinner who casts himself into the darkness by his very impenitence, just as it is I myself who dash myself in pieces if I insist in walking over a precipice. The " second death " is a suicide's death.

There should be nothing in what has just been said which will be found incompatible with the sterner side of the New Testament teaching about the life to come. If we say that to be " lost " is to have no interests left in life, to have found everything very vanity of vanities and yet to be doomed to live on with nothing of which one has not grown utterly weary to live for, we are not chargeable with any weakly sentimental concern to hold out a comfortable prospect to the rebel and the " waster ". A partial illustration may be taken from the kind of wreck a man is sometimes seen to make of himself even in this earthly life. We sometimes see a man endowed with great gifts, capable of high things, and, at first, fired with an ardour for them, succumbing to an ignoble passion for a thoroughly worthless woman. His unhappy infatuation leads him to cut himself off from any effective pursuit of the worthier aims which appeal to all that is really best within him; he puts himself into a " false position " which leaves him nothing to live for but the woman to whom he has made the sacrifice, and then, often enough, when it is too late, he discovers that she has not been " worth it ", his " devotion " has been no more than " the expense of spirit in a waste of shame ". There is no way back to better things, and if there were, he has been so changed himself for the worse that he no longer feels the single-minded zest for them. He has years of life still before him and nothing but trivialities with which to fill them; he has nothing left to look forward to but self-contempt and *tædium vitæ*, or, at best, to escape the bitterness of this weary self-contempt, by dulling consciousness altogether and lowering himself, as far as it can be done, into a life of mere torpid vegetation. It would not make the ruin of his life any really the more tragic or the prospect of it any more appalling, to add the penalties of the " political sanction ", stripes and imprisonment. Apart from any such external consequences, it is the withered and wasted life itself which is its own true

" punishment ". " He gave them their heart's desire, and sent leanness withal into their souls."

A finally " lost " soul would be in the sort of position of which we have been speaking, only that its realization of the worthlessness of the objects of its past infatuation and the incomparable worth of all it has flung away in their pursuit must be thought to be even more clear-sighted, and there is not, if the soul is immortal, even the possibility of the cold comfort one might derive from the reflection that the aimless life will some day be closed by death, that " even the weariest river Winds somewhere safe to sea ". If we allow ourselves to entertain the merciful hope that at any rate the consciousness of the soul which has thus wasted the gift of intellect and will must eventually be dulled until it becomes a mere bare awareness of existence, the prospect remains unspeakably terrible, as the prospect of sinking into idiocy could be to a sane and active man. There is no need further to dishonour our God by representing Him as an ingenious contriver of tortures in order to justify the New Testament language about the " outer darkness ", and the " death " which is the " wages of sin ". The purpose of what we have said in the last few pages has been to keep our conception of God at the Christian level, not to offer a comfortable prospect to the evil-doer.[1]

[1] The men of the Middle Ages had, indeed, a quasi-rational ground for their insistence on physical, or quasi-physical, " torments ". They reasoned that as the debt contracted by evil-doing has been incurred by the whole man (soul and body together), justice requires that the penalty be also exacted from the whole man. The question which they did not face, and could hardly be expected to face, is this. Their theory required that it should be the *same* soul and the *same* body which concur in the transgression and share the penalty. But in what sense, beyond that of being an organ of expression to the same intellect and will, can a man's body be said to remain the same body, even

And we must be careful once more to remember that the evil-doer whose possible hopeless perdition it is salutary for me to bear in mind is not my neighbour but myself. As to my neighbours, Christianity has clearly forbidden presumptuous censoriousness, though bad Christians are perpetually forgetting the prohibition. It is always wrong for me to " deal damnation all around " on those whom I judge evil, because, if the full truth were known, at their worst they may actually be less flagrant offenders against the light they possess than I am against my own lights, and again, I do not know what changes may yet be wrought in them by the influences of God's grace. But for myself the really grave danger is that I may presume on my " final perseverance ", and allow myself to forget that self-complacency or indolence may yet bring me to utter undoing. Bunyan said that there was a way to hell even from the gates of the Celestial City. So there is, as all wise men know; but Christian should have bethought himself of the fact earlier, and as a caution to himself. It should not

during this life? If I commit a murder and am convicted and hanged for it twelve or fifteen years later, it is, I suppose, certain that the tissues of my body have been entirely renewed, perhaps more than once, in the interval; yet no one would contend that it is unjust that I should be hanged for the dead on the ground that no item of the body which suffers is identical with any item of that which carried out the murderer's intention. For the purposes of justice it is sufficient that the two systems of living matter are related by their relations to the same designing intellect and will, that it is the same *person* who offends and who suffers. Now on any theory this also holds good of the consequences of evil-doing in the unseen world; how personality expresses itself there, what precisely a " spiritual body " is, we do not know, but whatever it may be, it is the whole man, as he exists there, who reaps the consequences of his past life. The principle of the argument was sound, whatever we may think of the way it was applied. It is no part of my intention to advocate a Cartesian bisection of a person into a " pure spirit " on the one hand and a lump of " stuff " on the other.

have been brought in, too late, as a reflection upon a third party. We cannot be too careful to beware of the temper of spiritual arrogance which makes bold to anticipate the judgment of God by pronouncing that any of our neighbours have finally cut themselves off from salvation, but also we cannot too seriously remind ourselves, as a reason for vigilance and humility, that we *may* yet make the " great refusal " ourselves. When we try to imagine to ourselves the " day of doom ", we shall only do so to edification if we never allow ourselves to forget that the question which vitally concerns us is the old one: " What shall *I, frail man*, be pleading?"

But enough was said, perhaps, on the theme in an earlier paragraph. And in substance all that needs to be said is contained in the one apostolic question: How shall *we* escape if *we* neglect so great a salvation? The hope of which we have been trying to speak is a hope of a good transcending all our imagination, but it is still a hope which has to be held by each of us, as far as he is himself concerned, with " godly fear ", because he may always by his own wilfulness or carelessness frustrate his own fruition of it.[1] There is not one of us who can afford to

---

[1] This is the explanation of a sentence in the Burial Office of the English Church which has sometimes been amazingly misunderstood. It has been asked, even by those intelligent enough to know better, how it can be justifiable to say " we commit his body to the ground . . . in sure and certain hope " over a man whose life has been notoriously evil. The question answers itself if the quotation is not broken arbitrarily short. The *sure and certain* hope spoken of is that " of the resurrection to eternal life ". That the hope will be fulfilled in the case of the particular person over whose grave the words are said is not said to be sure and certain, and could not be said without presumption. The meaning is that we are assured of the reality of eternal life, and that in the particular case, even where appearances are least promising, we dare not pronounce hope to be excluded. If we did, we should be allowing " the parson " to take on himself to exercise the prerogative of his Creator.

disregard the same writer's warning against the irreparable false choice of " Esau, who for one morsel of meat sold his birthright ", only to discover when it was too late that the choice could not be recalled, or the similar admonition of a greater apostolic writer: " Hope to the end for the grace that is to be brought unto you at the revelation of Jesus Christ . . . but . . . pass the time of your sojourning here in fear." St. Paul tells us, in one of his most famous outbursts, of his confidence that " neither death, nor life, nor angels, nor principalities, nor powers, nor things present, nor things to come . . . nor any other creature can separate us from the love of God ". But there is one thing which he does not say; he does not say that we ourselves cannot, by our own refusal to respond to that love, effect the separation which is beyond the united powers of all things else in heaven and in earth. Even we ourselves, I have ventured to say, cannot put ourselves beyond that lovingkindness of our Creator which is over all His works; but we can cut ourselves off from that more intimate and special " love of God which is in Christ Jesus our Lord " towards those who are being re-made in His likeness; that self-separation is the " outer darkness " of those who are excluded from eternal life. If we dare not affirm of any of our fellows that he has brought that exclusion on himself, neither dare any of us affirm of himself that he may not yet do so.

Vigilemus et oremus.

INDEX